Remembering NORCROSS

Remembering Norcross

Nuggets of Nostalgia

SALLY TOOLE

Published by The History Press
Charleston, SC 29403
www.historypress.net

Copyright © 2009 by Sally Toole
All rights reserved

Cover painting: A colorful scene of downtown, by Norcross native and artist Florence Warbington Green. *Courtesy of Anita Andrews.*

First published 2009

ISBN 9781540219565

Library of Congress Cataloging-in-Publication Data

Toole, Sally.
Remembering Norcross : nuggets of nostalgia / Sally Toole.
p. cm.
ISBN 9781540219565
1. Norcross (Ga.)--History. 2. Norcross (Ga.)--Biography. I. Title.
F294.N6T66 2009
975.8'223--dc22
2009019600

Notice: The information in this book is true and complete to the best of our knowledge. It is offered without guarantee on the part of the author or The History Press. The author and The History Press disclaim all liability in connection with the use of this book.

All rights reserved. No part of this book may be reproduced or transmitted in any form whatsoever without prior written permission from the publisher except in the case of brief quotations embodied in critical articles and reviews.

Contents

Acknowledgements	7
Introduction	9
Feathers and Firewater	11
Shingles and Feathers—A Specialty	15
Northern Aggression	23
Running Rails over Indian Trails	29
A Mirror of the Past	35
Holy Row	57
Atlanta's Favorite Summer Resort	61
Apple Pie, Baseball and Norcross	65
Brothers in Baseball	69
Bottle Caps and Broomsticks, Nulling Tops and Taw Lines	75
Storefronts	81
Shootouts	87
Hope Wells from Slavery's Shackles	93
From Books to Bandages to Bazaars	103
Pioneer Paean	109
A Simple Story	113
Pasture Golf	115
Home Shine	117
Apothecaries and Cemeteries	123
About the Author	127

Acknowledgements

It is my privilege to share the stories of many Norcross folks I have happily called my "neighbors" for more than twenty-five years. A special thanks to members of the Norcross Old Timers Baseball Association for their many interviews and sincere help.

Not wanting to leave anyone out, I do send a gracious thank-you to Martha Simpson Nesbit, Carl and Joan Garner, Colonel John Adams, Evelyn "Bud" Norman, Ralph Simpson, Rufus Dunnigan, Anne Barker, Craig Newton, Anita Andrews, Ralph Simpson, Wanda Snyder, Bob Warbington, Anne Webb, Joy and Jim Nesbit, Lillian Webb and Hattie McClendon. I hope to honor the memory of Martha Miller Adams, Florence Warbington Green and Avery Graves, all of whom I enjoyed speaking with in life.

I appreciate Dan Roper, editor of *Georgia Backroads Magazine*, and Ray Cobb, editor of *Inside Gwinnett Magazine*, for the outlets they provide.

A big thank-you to Clifton "Buddy" Ray for sharing treasured diary excerpts.

I send a gracious acknowledgement for the wonderful prose of Alice Youngblood.

Consideration is given to the many helpful folks of Norcross City Hall; the Norcross Station Café; gracious members of Mount Carmel Methodist, Hopewell and Norcross First Baptist Churches; Norcross Woman's Club; Forty-second Georgia Infantry reenactors; and the Southeastern Railway Museum.

Love and thanks to my husband Mark, who shares my enthusiasm for history.

A special "back at you" to our children, Mark Jr., Will and Lily, and their many friends who have shown interest and enthusiasm, real or imagined, in the stories I tell and retell at the kitchen table when all they really wanted was a chicken wing.

Introduction

A train whistle blows distant from the south. Soft at first listen, then it crescendos to a dish-rattling rumble assuring denizens that all is as it should be, as it has been, in Norcross, Georgia, for more than one hundred years. Since 1866, children have scrambled alongside the tracks anxious to catch a glimpse of strong black engines powering past homes, churches and businesses. Their eyes shine with excitement as enormous as the steel wheels squealing to pull lorry, tanker, box, flat and hopper cars, coupled together in a mile-long procession northward. Although the trains no longer stop at the Norcross depot, no longer turntable or reverse themselves back to the south, no longer pick up or drop off passengers or goods or bags of mail and money, their bellow shakes, like feathers on a hawk, the imagination of those within eye- or earshot.

With few interruptions, save several days following September 11, 2001, the rhythm of a train trumpeting short blasts and long blows sounds an abiding sonance. For babes, the trill rocks a soothing lullaby. For old-timers, the whistle whines of days gone by, when early settlers mingled, for the most part, in harmonious accord with Creek and Cherokee Indians as both cultures worshipped their creator, farmed their land, traded their goods, birthed their young and buried their dead.

Narrative nuggets, dug up in diaries, deeds and death certificates, connect the doings of the deceased.

Anne Webb of the Save Historic Norcross Preservation Society wrote the following:

> *Norcross residents found more than a friend when Derek Norcross of Hastings, England discovered the city named for his famous forebear,*

Introduction

Many residents remember Norcross as a bustling Georgia whistle stop. *Courtesy of Anita Andrews.*

Jonathan Norcross, first mayor of Atlanta. Our city found a legacy, connecting with the family of its famous namesake still living in England. Both Derek and Jonathan trace roots to Norcross Manor in the north of England. "Norcross" is Viking in origin meaning "Men of the North Cross."

Mr. Norcross discovered our town by accident in the early 1980's while on a speaking tour in the United States, lecturing on the performing arts. After September 11, 2001, when many were afraid to fly, Mr. Norcross came to speak at the new Norcross High School dedication. Derek spoke of how life moves in circles. He called his discovery of the town that shares his name "the completing of a circle." Again in 2003 Mr. Norcross came to open the British Heritage Crowns and Regalia Exhibition in Thrasher Park. His enthusiasm for our city was infectious. In one conversation of the struggle to save the old Methodist church, circa 1875 and a focal point of the historic district, he said, "You absolutely must save it! You have to change the thinking of those who want to tear down the town's history!"

Feathers and Firewater

Exposed to European culture when Spanish explorers landed in La Florida in the 1500s, passive and aggressive tribes of American Indians freely grouped in communities to trade and council with one another for hundreds of years throughout the southeastern United States. An Ocheessee Creek confederacy—Ocheessee being an English given name for a tribe that lived near the Ocmulgee River—was composed of, among others, Creek, Cherokee, Choctaw and Oconee, a total of twelve tribes in all.

Councils squatted deep within sacred mounds, built by their ancestors in 2500 BC, or tethered their canoes together at points of river conversions, like the spot on the Chattahoochee River that Indians called "Standing Pitch tree." Pitch trees are a type of pine whose sap the natives learned to extract and use to seal leaks in their canoes. Chattahoochee, translated "shallow place," is a large river that had to be crossed by both the Indians and the earliest of Spanish and English settlers.

James Oglethorpe, a member of the English Parliament in 1722, had the idea of creating a colony of debtors in the New World. A group of twenty-one men, including Oglethorpe and Lord John Viscount Percival, created a charter for Georgia in honor of King George II. The grant included all land between the Altamaha and Savannah Rivers and from the headwaters of these rivers to the "south seas." The charter specifically prohibited rum and slavery.

In 1789, Georgia voters participated in the first U.S. presidential election. As a result of the war of 1812, Fort Daniel was erected in Hog Mountain, Georgia, roughly thirty-five miles north of present-day Atlanta, to protect early settlers in Gwinnett County from the Cherokee tribes that did not engage in the friendly trade of "feathers and firewater" with anyone except the British with whom they remained loyal. A "road," no more than a wide dirt path, beginning at the fort on Hog Mountain, was needed to transport goods and soldiers to a shallow ford of the Chattahoochee, near the Terminus area (now Atlanta), in order to develop the railroad system for a newly annexed South.

The officer whose duty it became to construct this road was Captain Nehemiah Garrison, the first commander of the fort. Garrison procured the services of Robert Young, Isham Williams and William Nesbit, all of whom were local stock raisers familiar with the Indian markings they would follow along a natural ridge to the mouth of Suwannee Creek, where the new fort was to be built. Indians bent the trunks of young oaks by strapping them with strips of hide, forcing the trunks to grow in a distinctive "elbow" to point out paths. Closest to Norcross is the Hightower Trail, running parallel to the Eastern Continental Divide. The divide is a watershed ridge running from Florida to New York State that separates the flow of rain to either the Atlantic Ocean or a more westward runoff to the Gulf of Mexico. This ridge was well tracked by Indian trails and later by the railroad. Tribes spent some nine hundred years becoming familiar with this higher ground, which allowed them to avoid large river crossings and rougher terrain as they traveled. Along these trails, Indians carved out picture messages in beech trees, referred to as "witness trees," intending for these "notes" to be "read" by other Indians who passed, often warning them about rattlesnakes or white men. The beech tree proved perfect for this purpose, as its bark did not grow over the etchings with the passing of time.

William Nesbit began the task of marking the road in 1813. A young man, Nesbit was swift of foot, proving himself helpful in many circumstances, such as when the group, making its way along the trail, was confronted by a wild turkey, disabled by one injured wing, which stepped out in front of them. Nesbit took off after it. Success was rewarded with a fire-roasted fowl for dinner. Once initial markings were made for the soon to be dug road, the three men furnished several hired hands, including Bob Young, Lewis Lawly, his brother John Lawly and a Negro man (as it was written in a remembrance of Judge Wynn in 1873), to do the work of final construction of the ten-foot-wide Pitch Tree Road. Young traveled in front of the group on picket duty, scouting out redskins who might be on the warpath. The men mounted their horses and rode off ahead to waylay a possible surprise attack. Evening fell on one such night, finding the men around a campfire preparing a dinner meal. As they ate, they were startled by a clear and shrill ring of "whoop, whoop, whoopee!" The alarmed settlers dumped their tin coffee cups as they jolted to their feet. Soon galloping horses neared the campsite and a

Nuggets of Nostalgia

A bent tree Indian trail marker still standing at the base of Stone Mountain, Georgia, is most likely more than three hundred years old. *Author's collection.*

voice called out for Nesbit. The voice of Young was quickly recognized, to the relief of the work crew. Young admitted that the fearful "war whoop" had emanated from him, as recorded in his own words by Wynn, "a bit of mischief 't try the metal of the boys." Bob Young is described in the writings of Judge Wynn as a "character, the likes of whom have seldom been seen. He knew nothing of books, only the great book of nature. He was a man of superior sense and judgment, a man who had stored up, through observation, a wealth of knowledge invaluable to himself and the fellows around him. His word was a promise and his integrity never questioned. He tied his long hair back with a 'queue' that he prized and of which he proudly wore to the day of his death."

When the road that they named Pitch Tree was opened, the contractors received $150 for payment of their efforts. The road, through time and confusion, became "Peachtree Road," much to the chagrin of Atlanta navigators confused by an entanglement of highways with "Peachtree" in their names, such as West Peachtree, South Peachtree, North Peachtree, Peachtree DeKalb, Peachtree Corners, Peachtree Circle, Peachtree Dunwoody, Peachtree Industrial, Old Peachtree, New Peachtree and Peachtree Parkway.

William Nesbit helped to create Gwinnett, representing the county in Milledgeville, then the state capital, from 1829 to 1837. A line of his descendants settled in Norcross. He is remembered as a striking man, tall at a full six feet, of well-rounded proportion, evincing strength, with a walking carriage bespeaking manliness, yet kind and benevolent. Nesbit died June 27, 1863, at the age of seventy-six.

Eulogy of William Nesbit
I name them over one by one
And weep o'er days forever gone;
O'er friends whose suns of life have set
And voices thrilling memory yet,

They vanished like a morning beam
Or sunlight on the rippling stream;
And gloom lurks in the web of years
And hope of youth all disappears.

Shingles and Feathers—A Specialty

Many pioneer families ferried the incoming settlers, defended the South against Northern aggression, dug out the roads and laid the rails of a developing Gwinnett County, generation by generation, for nearly two hundred years.

Of the four settlements that eventually fed into the new town of Norcross, Pinckneyville became the largest and most organized, growing from an Indian trading post along the Eastern Continental Divide to a community of hearty pioneers.

A large north Georgia land expanse, once Indian Territory, now makes up four counties: Hall, Walton, Gwinnett and Habersham. The land was ceded to the United States in the Treaty of the Creek Agency, signed on January 22, 1818, between the United States and a gathering of Creek chiefs and warriors. A deal was struck in consideration of "certain sums of money" equaling, after eleven years of eleven payments, $120,000, and for three years, the use of "two blacksmiths and strikers."

Although the settlement was originally nicknamed "Buzzard's Roost" or "Turkey Gizzard," settlers collectively began calling their community "Pinckneyville" after an impressive visit from the South Carolina statesman Charles Pinckney, a three-time governor, minister to Spain, friend to Thomas Jefferson and gentleman who traveled the area sometime before 1850. "We have already taught some of the oldest and wisest nations to explore their rights as men," he once told fellow citizens.

Pinckneyville established a post office in 1828 and held inferior and militia court from that year until 1866.

As the first stop on the stagecoach line that ran westward from Savannah via Augusta, Pinckneyville was a travelers' rest, hosting visitors at the

A relic of an Indian chimney, built before 1800, located near the Simpson family farmhouse. *Author's collection.*

Pinckneyville Hunnicutt Inn. The inn, built and run by the Hunnicutt family, is said to have had a secret room used over the decades as a hiding place for Confederate soldiers or, some believe, gold. The secret room's true purpose remains a mystery.

The first church in the community, Mount Carmel Methodist, was organized in 1826 on a five-acre lot donated by Daniel Pittman. Washington Academy was established in 1827 to provide education for the children of the community on the property where Shiloh Baptist Church sits today on Spalding Drive. A second school, Crabapple Academy, was built near the present site of Pinckneyville Middle School, named in honor of the first settlement, and located on an apple orchard donated by the Westbrook family.

On July 12, 1833, the Goshen Presbyterian Church organized about four miles north of present-day Norcross on land donated by Thomas Hardaway Jones. As with most churches, services dwindled during the Civil War, and one visiting preacher was accused of being a spy for the Union. After Norcross became a town, this church building and land were

Nuggets of Nostalgia

Georgia was predominantly a farm community, and many folks saw one another at one of the many cotton mills in the county. *Courtesy of the Nesbit family.*

sold when the congregation thought it better to worship in town in the Methodists' sanctuary. The man who purchased it tore down the church and used the timbers to build a barn. He did not honor his debt to the congregation and they returned to the spot about 1900, slowly becoming known as Norcross Presbyterian.

In 1869, J.J. Thrasher purchased 250 acres around the proposed first stop north along the developing Richmond-Danville lines. The first depot was constructed a block or so south of its present-day location and became the center of the town that Thrasher was developing. In about 1900, the depot was moved closer to the intersecting main streets, Jones and South Peachtree.

Known as "Cousin John," Thrasher was born February 24, 1818, and spent his childhood in Newton County, Georgia. He was the son of David Thrasher, who lived in Georgia from 1796 to 1882.

Cousin John was only twenty-one when he came to an area that became southwest Atlanta. Hired to do work on the Western Atlantic Railroad,

Remembering Norcross

Likely the oldest home in town, 297 South Peachtree Street was built well before the fire of 1860, when recorded deeds were destroyed. *Courtesy of Evelyn Norman.*

Thrasher opened a general store near the location of the present-day First Presbyterian Church of Atlanta for the workers on his crew. He also built houses for the workers out of discarded slabs of wood milled for rail timbers, and the little shanty village and one store affectionately became known as Thrasherville.

Thrasher purchased an expanse of land in Whitehall, now the west end area, originally designated to be the "zero mile marker" for the railroad. Thrasher's plan for steady business at the general store generated by the railroad's terminal was dashed in 1842 when Lemuel P. Grant, a railroad employee, donated land to the railroad just northeast of Whitehall and the terminus was moved. A disgruntled Thrasher sold his land at a significant loss and moved to Griffin, Georgia.

Cousin John married in 1844 and returned to Atlanta, called "Marthasville" at that time, opening another store on Peachtree Street, across from the store of Jonathan Norcross, a man who quickly became Thrasher's best friend. Thrasher was active in local politics, becoming a state legislator representing Fulton County. The railroad's development was halted in 1861 as the Civil War began, and it wasn't until after the war was over and Atlanta had burned at the hands of General Sherman's troops as they "Marched to the Sea"

Nuggets of Nostalgia

that Thrasher became deeply involved in Atlanta politics. He spearheaded Atlanta's first jail, school and streetcars.

Thrasher told the Atlanta Historical Society in 1871,

> *When I arrived in this place in 1839, the country was entirely covered by forest. There was but one house here at the time…First one pioneer family moved in from the country and then another until we had a right smart little town. The people around here were very poor. There were a great many of the women who wore no shoes at all. We had dirt floors in our homes.*

Jonathan Norcross was born in Maine in 1808 and moved to Marthasville in 1844. As the Terminus area grew, its name was changed to Marthasville, until 1845, when it was again renamed as Atlanta. Four years later, Norcross built a store on part of half an acre of land he had purchased for $100 at the angle of two streets, where he hoped to catch passing trade. He is said to have offered customers "shingles and feathers—a specialty." The store was caddy corner from Thrasher's store and included a post office with a walk-up window opening out to a porch. The window allowed folks to pick up their mail while keeping the loafers and their muddy tracks out. His store remained at that location for many years, referred to by locals as "Norcross corner." This section of Atlanta was a location for the filming of the movie *Gone with the Wind*. Jonathan Norcross's store can be seen in the background of the scene in which "Big Sam" (a freed slave) tells Scarlett, "I'm goin' with the white soldiers to dig holes for them to hide in."

Mr. Norcross was successful as a dry goods merchant as well as a sawmill operator. An innovative businessman, he filed the U.S. Patent 3210 for the first "reciprocating saw" in August 1843. His sawmill produced cross ties and string timbers for the railroad.

Even as the railroad continued to develop Terminus, some folks just didn't believe that the town would amount to much. It is recorded that on November 3, 1840, the chief engineer of the W&A Railroad resigned his position and left, saying, "The Terminus is good for one tavern, one blacksmith shop, a grocery store, and nothing else." The engineer is recorded to have rejected an offer for two hundred acres of land that is now Marietta Street, near the vicinity Atlanta residents call Little Five Points.

Most of the characters in town were known to be rough and rowdy except for the two businessmen and friends, Thrasher and Norcross, who actively developed positive aspects of the community. Norcross donated slabs of wood from milled railroad ties for railroad workers to build homes in an area called "slab town." Thrasher extended credit to many patrons of his store,

This postcard advertises the "specialties" offered by a photographer on Whitehall Street. *Courtesy of the Nesbit family.*

once giving a generous gift of cash and staples to relatives who rode into town. One story recalls a distant cousin of Thrasher sending his daughters to trade cotton for goods. When Thrasher realized that they were relatives, so the story goes, the girls were given more goods than was the value of the cotton they came to trade. Thrasher was not concerned with the discrepancy, but the girls insisted on paying the balance by producing a "gold coin" from an unknown source.

The two entrepreneurs became well known for their civic contributions and quickly threw their hats into the political arena. Thrasher was a state representative from 1859 through 1863, and Norcross was elected the fourth mayor of Atlanta. Thrasher lobbied successfully to move the Georgia state capital from Milledgeville to Atlanta.

Little is known of the activities of these two men during the Civil War, but during Reconstruction work on the railways began in earnest and the two friends became deeply involved in all aspects of its completion. Thrasher was interested in moving his family out of the city of Atlanta, so he purchased land lot No. 254, which consisted of about 250 acres surrounding the new train stop. He promptly divided this land into lots and sold them at auction. Gathering four councilmen, with himself elected as the first mayor, Thrasher named the new town Norcross for Jonathan, his longtime friend. The city

Nuggets of Nostalgia

of Norcross was incorporated on October 26, 1870, sparking a migration of settlers eager to build "in town" homes and open "in town" businesses.

Another Norcross-born businessman, Edward F. Buchanan, was instrumental in the town's continued economic growth through a variety of successful ventures. Buchanan was adopted in 1871, only a few days old, by Mr. and Mrs. Leslie Buchanan, who, if they ever knew who his true parents were, never revealed the secret. The Buchanan family was not wealthy and could only offer young Edward the basics. He attended only two years of formal schooling and began working at the age of ten inside the train depot. When still a boy, Buchanan became so proficient in operating the telegraph that he could tap outgoing messages with his right hand while receiving messages with his left. At the formative age of thirteen, Buchanan left the only home he had ever known, Norcross, to travel west, finding work as a telegraph operator. He returned to Norcross sometime in the 1890s while in the employment of the Atlanta branch of the Western Union Telegraph Company.

A great beauty and former model, Miss Bertie Redwine, married the successful Buchanan and moved with him to New York City as he entered into the services of Hudson & Company as an operator. He rose quickly as a most qualified stockbroker. He was taken on as a junior partner at the cotton brokerage of A.O. Brown. During the early 1900s, the couple was associating with an exclusive society crowd, living much of the time at the Waldorf Astoria Hotel in Manhattan.

By the age of thirty-seven, Edward Buchanan, a boy abandoned while not yet dry behind the ears, became a millionaire.

With a tender spot for Norcross, the Buchanans returned to his birthplace in a private Pullman car, often coupled to the lavish cars of his millionaire friends, eighteen to twenty at a time, who sought to enjoy the resort atmosphere that Norcross had become famous for.

In 1905, Buchanan began building a striking gray granite stone mansion at the northwest corner of Thrasher Park for his foster mother, S.P. Buchanan Tedder. During construction, granite blocks were shipped in by rail from Stone Mountain, Georgia, where massive ledges of granite were actively carved out from 1840 to 1950. These blocks were pre-cut and were individually numbered to be replaced in matching order. The cost to build and furnish the home was an estimated $40,000, a sizeable investment, as he added every elaborate modern touch, including electricity and indoor plumbing, which were not available in town. Buchanan established the Norcross waterworks and electric lighting plants specifically for his mother's convenience in the mansion, and by 1907, neighbors were offered the option of "hooking on" to the system at no cost.

Remembering Norcross

Over his most prosperous years, Buchanan began the Buchanan Plow and Implement Company at a cost of $100,000, creating a great number of jobs in Norcross. He also began an automotive manufacturing plant in Norcross and a company that produced a type of Morse code telegraph known as the "Vibrex."

The automobile, called a "Nor-X," was the first car ever manufactured in Georgia. Sales were limited to his wealthy northern friends, and upon the car's maiden drive it was discovered that the gears had been incorrectly installed and the car only traveled in reverse. Although this transmission issue was resolved, sales of the Nor-X never took off.

Generous to a fault, Buchanan purchased a zebra named Buck for the Grant Park Zoo in Atlanta; sent a crippled boy for treatments, eventually considering the child his "adopted" son; gave warm clothing to newsboys; paid medical expenses for his employees; and curiously gave children cash for every June bug they brought to him, as he frowned upon their childish game of tying a string to their legs and flying them like a kite. Edward donated $400 to the Uncle Remus Memorial Fund.

Returning to live in New York, Buchanan divorced Miss Redwine and married Lillian Keith, a wealthy lady from Chicago.

In 1908, the company of which he was a partner folded just days before he and his partners were arrested for "fraudulent transactions." The legal scramble left him with only an $8,000 interest in a Prescott, Arizona gold mine. On his way to stir investor interest in the mine, he suffered a stroke and returned to his foster mother's home in Norcross to recover. Forced to return to work at Western Union, Buchanan suffered a heart attack and died in 1910 at Grady Memorial Hospital in Atlanta. An Atlanta bank discovered a balance of $70 in his account at the time of his death.

After his years of philanthropic gestures, the city of Norcross welcomed the penniless son home to rest. Not comfortable with the generous soul being buried in an unmarked pauper's grave, Buchanan lies in the plot of his adoptive family below an engraved stone donated by the Sunday school class of Norcross First Methodist Church.

Northern Aggression

While Gwinnett County pioneers of Pinckneyville, Flint Hill, Beaver Ruin and Mechanicsville districts were settling into contented lives tilling the soil, raising their children, attending church and visiting with neighbors, war clouds were brewing. The questions of slavery and taxation were coming to a head between the states north and south of the Mason-Dixon line. A misnomer of history is the belief that the Civil War was a valiant effort on the part of Northern states, standing behind Abraham Lincoln, to free the Southern Negro slaves owned by, a point somewhat skewed by history, "every white man in the south." In truth, a mere 7 to 10 percent of Southern affluent "plantation" owners, most having interests and holdings in the railroad and the politics of trade, truly owned or sold humans as possessions. It is a fact that several Northern states had no anti-slave laws, with farmers of those states also owning families of Africans plucked from their ancestral homes and shipped to the continental United States with other "cargo."

In 1861, Georgia senator Robert Toombs gave his farewell speech to the U.S. Senate warning that if Northern states refused to grant Southern states their constitutional rights, "We shall then ask you 'Let us depart in peace.' Refuse that, and you present us war. We accept it; and inscribing upon our banners the glorious words, 'Liberty and Equality,' we will trust in the blood of the brave and the God of Battles for security and tranquility." Many young men born to the earliest settlers in Georgia enlisted to serve in a conflict that they perceived as an aggression of the North infringing on states' rights. They believed that the Federal government was taxing them without an equal legislative voice in the House of Representatives. Even the dirt poor Southern farmer felt an economic pinch from tariffs, voted

Confederate troops fire weapons from a drill line. *Courtesy of the Forty-second Regiment of Georgia reenactors.*

into law by Northern politicians, that raised taxes, and therefore prices, on everyday goods shipped into Florida, Georgia and the Carolinas from Europe. The tariffs forced Southerners to purchase goods from Northern states at a higher cost.

Men, young and old, white farmers and freed Negroes, left mothers, wives and children alone to work the farm and dodge the devastating path that Union troops seared across Georgia, to join the Confederacy. During the conflict, membership in the Washington Lodge of Free and Accepted Masons nearly doubled, with many members receiving all of their degrees of membership at a single session while home on furlough. Dr. Moses Richardson, also a farmer in an area that would later become Norcross, was a Confederate army surgeon, and while he was away for service his home was ransacked by the Yankees, who took anything they could find, including his Masonic apron. The officers failed to condemn the plundering but, upon seeing the apron, went to the house, where Richardson's petrified family explained that he was indeed a member of the order. After hearing this news, officers ordered their men to return all they had taken. The Yankees were served coffee with compliments from the officer in charge. D.P. McDaniel, a

Nuggets of Nostalgia

Soldiers break down doors of Southern plantations pillaging for supplies. *Courtesy of the Forty-second Regiment of Georgia reenactors.*

worshipful master during wartime, feared that the lodge would be destroyed and took all the lodge paraphernalia to his home for safe keeping. A Yankee squad came to rob the home but found Lodge regalia and left without taking anything. Before the family of Mason Burgess Kelly left their home to hide from the Union siege, they painted the Mason emblem on their door. Upon their return, the family found the home intact.

The men of the Ray family left women behind to attend to the farm. A story retold in diary writings remembers Sarah Ray, alone with a six-week-old infant to care for, walking from Norcross to Lawrenceville, a fifteen-mile trek one way, once a week for a peck of cornmeal. "Grandma" Sarah hid the few chickens, and possibly a hog, from the bands of pilfering soldiers that regularly trampled through Norcross. Sarah's son, Tom, just seven years old when Sherman marched across the Chattahoochee River less than five miles north of Norcross in 1864, daringly followed behind the Northern troops as they pillaged the silos of local farms. Tom would pick up ears of corn as they fell from the Yankee wagons, no doubt filling his pants, pockets and stockings with the cobs. Sarah's husband, John W. Ray, left home in March 1862 and did not return to the family farm until April 1865. As a result of injuries,

Remembering Norcross

John had trouble tending his farm, so family papers reveal that many aunts and uncles came to live on the farm along the dirt road that would become North Peachtree Street in downtown Norcross. John and Sarah were able to conceive John Aaron, born less than a year after the war ended, and another son, Marion Wesley, the diligent author of many journals that he entitled *A Mirror of the Past*.

Stephen Tilley McElroy was only a boy on November 18, 1862, when he enlisted with the Thirtieth Georgia Regiment, Reynolds Brigade, and Stevenson Division Army of Tennessee. His regiment campaigned in Vicksburg, Mississippi, during May 1863, and McElroy, hit once in the left leg and once on his left side, was stranded overnight among the carnage on the battlefield. The next day, Union and Confederate lines reformed and McElroy found himself lying defenseless beneath the ensuing fray. When at last comrades dragged him from the arena, his left leg was amputated "quickly"; skilled surgeons could do the task in three minutes, with no more anesthetic than a sip of whiskey, if the patient was lucky. After some recuperation in the home of a sympathetic Southern woman, McElroy made his way back to Jackson, Mississippi, but found the railroad tracks leading home torn up, presumably by Union troops. In Jackson, he joined a small group of Confederates making their way by ox cart to a prisoner of war camp in Denapolis, Alabama, where he was paroled. He reached Atlanta on July 4, 1863, the same day that Confederate troops surrendered at Vicksburg. McElroy returned to his family's farm and a house his family had built before the war broke out. Although Sherman scouted the area of Peachtree Street that runs through present-day Norcross, his troops did not burn the home, spotting a Masonic emblem painted on the door. The original shell of that farmhouse, passed down through six generations, has seen many structural changes, and is now a large events facility known as Flint Hill.

Most pathetic and sad of Norcross's Civil War stories may be the death of Hilliard Clark Jones. Jones was the youngest son of Thomas Hardaway Jones, who had seven older sons enlisted for the Confederacy who returned unscathed from war. Hilliard was a boy of eleven years when on January 30, 1864, one of his older brothers stopped by to visit the family's farm with a Confederate brigade under his command. The regiment was surprised by Federal troops, and a skirmish ensued. Hilliard was shot in the crossfire and died less than a mile from the Norcross city cemetery, in which he is interred. A stone plaque, illegible from the ravages of time and weather, marks his grave but no longer tells his story.

Allen W. Key served as a private in Company C, Thirty-sixth Georgia Infantry. He enlisted on March 3, 1862, in Dalton, Georgia, and was wounded the next year at Champion's Hill, Mississippi, on May 16. Prisoner of war registers show him as being left in a hospital there and then exchanged to a camp in Fort Delaware, Delaware, in June. After his release from the war camp, he returned to Atlanta, where he died in 1864, a result of lasting injuries and infection. His wife, Harriett, died in Norcross in 1865, leaving their child, Sarah Ann, an orphan who was adopted by her Uncle James Key.

James Hammrick, along with his brother-in-law John Ray, joined company K, Thirty-sixth Georgia Infantry. The Thirty-sixth, stationed at Camp Big Creek Gap, Tennessee, participated in the Tennessee campaign, but the company's largest engagement was at the siege of Vicksburg. The town sat helplessly surrounded by Yankees for several weeks under the command of General Grant. Reduced to near starvation, the desperate men were forced to eat mule meat. Ray was wounded in the leg but did not lose the limb. James was captured, and upon signing an Oath of Allegiance to the United States of America, he returned to Georgia to reenlist. He was killed in Jonesboro trying to stem Sherman's efforts to encircle Atlanta. He is buried there, quite possibly under a pointed marker, an effort, some say, by Southern stone carvers of that era to "keep them 'Damn Yankees from sittin' on the graves of our fallen Confederate heroes."

> *Prisoner of War Oath and Declaration of Allegiance to the United States of America*
>
> *I do solemnly swear that I will support, protect, and defend the Constitution and Government of the United States of America against all enemies, domestic or foreign, that I will bear true faith, allegiance, and loyalty, to the same, any ordinance, resolution or laws of any state, convention or legislature to the contrary not-with-standing; and further that I will faithfully perform all of the duties which might be required of me by the laws of the United States; and I take this oath freely and voluntarily, without mental reservation or evasion whatsoever. And further, I pledge my parole of honor to remain within the loyal states until permitted to go elsewhere by the Secretary of War.*

Many Confederate prisoners subscribed to and swore this oath, and were subsequently released from war camp. Many of these released prisoners rejoined the fight on the side of the Southern states.

Running Rails over Indian Trails

Georgia's first rail tracks were laid in the mid-1830s on routes leading from Athens, Augusta, Macon and Savannah. The Georgia Railroad was completed to Terminus—renamed Atlanta—in 1845. The rail scouts marked the lines to follow the same ridge line, the same Indian trails into which roads were being dug. When the Civil War broke out, lasting from 1861 to 1865, Atlanta was a rail hub for the Confederacy as locomotive transportation aided in troop movement and in the supplying of medical bags and weaponry, including muskets, swords, pistols, rifles and carbines. Therefore, the city was a key military target of Abraham Lincoln's Union to the north.

By 1850, Georgia had more miles of laid rails than any other southern state. The Richmond & Danville opened a 140-mile rail line between the two cities of its name in 1856. A 48-mile extension from Danville to Greensboro, North Carolina, was completed during the Civil War. After the war, the railroad line was to become a key link in the Piedmont Air Line, a system of railroads across the Southeast.

During the years of southern Reconstruction, railroad expansion led to town expansion as section crews flocked to work, and Norcross was no exception. By 1877, men, both black and white and hailing from Norcross as well as those who had traveled here for the ready work, used mules, plows and the strength of their backs to dig trenches, lay tracks and pound spikes into steel rails. To a melodious "old South" rhythm they hammered down a spider's web of steel rails across the state. Crews of work gangs were housed along the tracks in little towns springing up along the path of the rails. Such section houses sprang up behind the storefronts of Jones Street along Railroad Street, at first just a trenched pathway straddling the northbound track, over which folks drove their wagons, buggies or automobiles. Norcross's original one track, the commuter line of the Airline Belle, grew to two tracks, one running north and the other running south, with a side track that cut down and away from the main track. The side track lay in front of the depot and stopped just at the rear of Mrs. McKinney's corner dry goods building at 7 Jones Street, a brick building constructed by Riley Owen "R.O." Medlock in a style that railroad men refer to as a "standard" rail building. The proprietor could load and unload livestock, cotton bales or dry goods directly onto a large scale in the rear of the store, making it easy to weigh the incoming items upon their arrival.

A great number of Norcross men had railroad careers with the Southern, the Atlanta and Charlotte Air, the Airline Belle commuter, the Richmond-Danville, the Piedmont Limited and the Crescent Limited rail lines. Captain Frank Marshall began working on a section gang in 1877 at the age of twenty, advancing to a position as conductor in 1892. Pope Barrow conducted for the Southern Railroad for more than forty years and was on the Crescent

Built by R.O. Medlock in 1880, 7 Jones Street housed the millinery of Mrs. C.A. McKinney; a side track once ran along the west side. *Courtesy of Evelyn Norman.*

Nuggets of Nostalgia

Limited when it rolled its first rail. Thomas A. Rainey, born in Norcross in 1866, just four years before its incorporation, worked the Toccoa line, which became wildly popular for Atlanta area folks seeking a getaway to the beauty of the north Georgia mountains.

Homer Jones conducted on the Southern Railroad and was, on occasion, in charge of the freight trains that linked for several miles. With him on this task was friend and fellow Norcross native Horace Johnson, who served as flagman. The two often spoke of trouble on the long lines with robbers and hobos being found in the boxcars. The railroad company issued strict orders for conductors to "walk the line" several times during a run and report back to the flagman. After one such walk, Horace questioned Homer and he reported, "There was one fellow on down back a ways but after we got to talking I realized he was a relative and I didn't have the heart to make him get off. I wish you would walk back and do it for me."

Horace agreed and set off to extricate the tramp, who proved disagreeable, brandishing a pistol at the flagman. When Horace returned to the conductors' caboose, Homer asked if he was able to remove the stowaway.

"Nope," Homer replied. "I found out he was kin to me too."

During the Depression of the 1920s, the boxcars became transportation to the impoverished men who, unable to find work, became bums along the rails. On Railroad Street in Norcross, several section homes sat just off the sidetrack of the southern line. The bums and hobos often sought nothing more than a sip of coffee or a bite of food from the good people living in these homes. Norcross was still primarily a farm town then and most folks had plenty to eat. Many who lived in these track houses recall the desperate look in the eyes of the men who humbly rapped on their doors, forced to beg for a meager handout.

Irene Ewing Crapo was just a little girl during those difficult years, but she clearly remembers

> *It was hard to make a living then. We would fish in the river, pick blackberries and my brothers would hunt for rabbit and squirrel. We were lucky to get by. Some of our relatives had to come and stay with us until, as my mother would say, they could "get back on their feet." Dad always had a job and others did not so they would stay with us for weeks at a time, often with many children sleeping on "pallets," just blankets spread on the floor.*

When the Richmond-Danville became the Norfolk Southern, the second northbound track was removed, along with the sidetrack. The section homes of the train gangs were sold as private cottages along Railroad, now named

REMEMBERING NORCROSS

The Norcross train depot was a popular gathering spot for many decades, including this gang of guys who hung out there in the 1950s. *Courtesy of Carl and Joan Garner.*

Wingo, Street. Irene's parents, Nora Terrell and Bob Ewing, lived beside that stretch of tracks their entire married life, appropriate to how they met during World War I.

Irene's mother, Nora Terrell, had gone with her friend, Mary Lankford, to watch trainloads of troops pass through town, often waving flags or shouting encouragements to the boys destined to ship out. The two were along the section of tracks near Born and Railroad Streets when several of the soldiers threw out scraps of paper on which they had written their names and addresses. The soldiers would holler to the girls, skirts and hair flapping in the breeze of the passing engine, "Please write to me while I am away fighting the enemy!" Mary picked up several of the notes and handed one to Nora, saying, "Why don't you write to him…he looks interesting."

Nora corresponded with Bob for two years while he served overseas. Through letters, they agreed to be married. Ewing returned on the ship the *Leviathan* and was discharged in Montana. From there, he took a job herding sheep south.

With a jingle in his pocket, Bob returned to Norcross on August 14, 1919, where he and Nora met for the first time on the steps of the depot. On that same day the couple asked Dr. O.O. Simpson, owner of the only automobile in town, to drive them to Lawrenceville, the county seat, where they were married. The pair set up housekeeping in a tent on Railroad, now Wingo, Street, eventually building their home on the lot with Bob's war bonus of $100. Although Nora's brothers teased that Bob was a "ferrener" (a foreigner)

Nuggets of Nostalgia

Dr. O.O. Simpson, a notoriously poor driver, had one of the first and, for many years, only automobiles in town. *Courtesy of Evelyn Norman.*

and not familiar with the ways of the South, she stood by her husband for fifty-seven years until, in death, she departed in 1976.

During the 1950s, fewer trains stopped in town, so folks just hung out at the depot, mostly because there wasn't much else to do until evening fell anyway. After dark, the traffic on Highway 141 died down and the depot gang revved up the big engines of the era's fast Pontiacs, Fords and Chevys to race one another up and down the deserted stretch of road just a mile from the center of Norcross, an activity that, like barnyard distilleries, was mostly overlooked by local law enforcement.

A Mirror of the Past

Marion Wesley Ray worked as a formally educated teacher for a short time, but returned to help plow and harvest his Uncle T.B.'s farm "place," as he describes it, just a few steps from the center of town. Ray recorded his thoughts with pencil on 4½- by 8½-inch notepads, glued or sewn at the top. Some of the journal's bindings separated, leaving pages out of order or missing altogether. A transcription was started by Clifton V. "Buddy" Ray Jr., Marion's grandson, in August 1984, with grateful assistance in proofreading from Ordy P. Ray, Marion's daughter-in-law.

1896

Jan. 1, Having traveled all day on Yesterday from home, my nephew, Walter Ray, & myself find ourselves this morning at Mr. Birds in Dawson Co. 12 m. North of Cumming Ga. and 35 m. from home. Yesterday we crossed Chattahoochee river at Medlock's bridge, traveled through Milton and Forsythe Cos. We passed through the town of Cumming, a nice place, mountains to the North. We were intertained last night in the best of style by Miss Georgia Bird and brother Truman. This morning we have corn bread for breakfast but wine for the stomach. Miss Georgia seems to hate being just out of flour. Mrs Bird charges us .75 but I jew her to .50 because we had our own horse feed.

Jan. 1 It is very cool today, but the lantern at our feet helps very much. We passed through Dawson into Lumpkin Co. into the mountains where Stock Law is no more and the Razorback roams free.

Marion Wesley Ray authored journals detailing his life as a farmer. *Courtesy of Clifton Ray.*

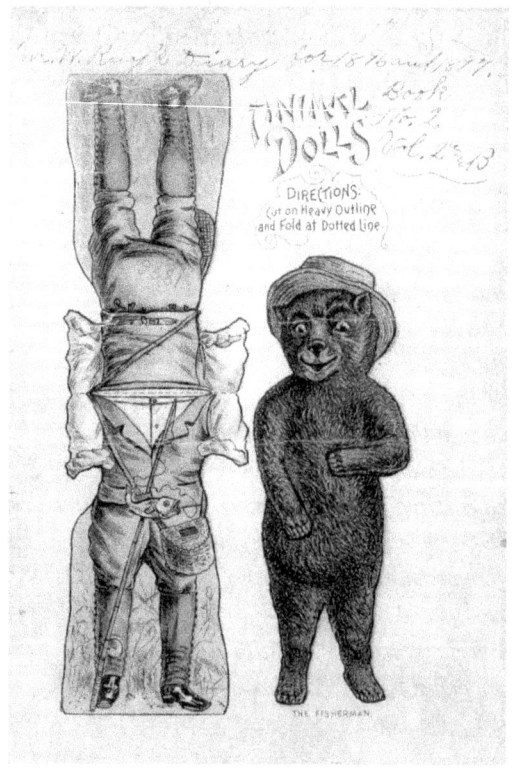

Paper doll cuts of a fishing bear were a bonus on the cover of this notebook Marion started in 1886. *Courtesy of Clifton Ray.*

Nuggets of Nostalgia

We pass the Gold mines and see the men at work, one shaft right by the road. Dahlonega a pretty town on an elevated plateau surrounded by mountains on all sides. We cross one creek seven times within a half mile. The houses are very scarce, we travel first around one mountain then another.

We stop for the night at Willow, Mr. Tates. Mr. T. has a very pretty daughter, Miss Sallie. We have the best of treatment.

Jan. 2, Mr. Tate, charges us .60 a fine breakfast, a big dish full of hog brains. We travel to-day through the grandest scenery I ever beheld. We cross the Chestatee river, then along at the foot of the great towering Blue Ridge Mts. across the Tesnatee river, and then we begin to climb up through Tesna Gap. Walter & I walk and urge Morgan up the winding pike. On the one side a towering wall on the other a yawning precipice, sheer down with Testnatee plunging down from crag to crag at the bottom.

We halt for dinner half way up the mountain. It looks like bad weather back down South. On top of the Mt. what a grand scene every where, every way. Sublime Mountains, Mountains everywhere.

Dark overtakes us 5m away but we keep driving on over the rough Mt. road, the night is very dark, the clouds come heavy and the rain begins to drop down But at last the welcome sight of the flickering lights of Young Harris come to view, and soon we are by the bright blasing fire of Mr. W.N. Hunnicutt's. We are just ninety miles away from home, the fartherest in life

Jan. 3, One thing that I see in the Mts. country reminds me of my early childhood, that is the many flocks of sheep, the tinkle of bells and baa can be heard on all sides. Apples, apples the very finest from 20 to 30 cents per bu. Mine host keeps me eating continually of this luscious fruit. In the P.M. I meet Dr. Irwin. On invitation I room at night with a student Mr. Reeves of Ashville, N.C.

Jan. 4, I start for home to-day. Mr. Hunnicutt comes with me, I am glad to have company over the Mts. and through the lonesome foothills. We start about Sunup it is very cold the creeks being frozen over. We stop and see a large flat rock upon which has been cut the tracks of different kind of animals, bear, deer, wolf, fox, cow, horse, cat, dog, sheep, man etc. These tracks were cut by the Indians how long ago we know not. We stop for dinner at Mr. Jack Hood's in Chosecolly valley, foot of Blue Ridge (N. side) Mr. Hood has lived here in the same house since before the Cherokees were removed. The Mt. girls up here are the pictures of health, nature at her very best, the acme of her glory. Red cheeks, rosy lips and sparkling eyes that make a man feel—well I can't describe it. Not all, however, are mountain tulips or Lily of the Valley, for I past one house in Union Co. where a red faced, golden haired girl put her head out the door. While her long muscular nose was pointing direct at me one eye was on a bee line up the road and the other was looking straight down the road, I whipped up my horse to get away from such uncertainty. And I also met a man in Union who was so crosseyed he couldn't get his horse past our buggy, swore he would have to go back to Blairsville (7m) and turn around. The people living along the Blue Ridge are the poorest & most ignorant set of squatters I ever saw. In the P.M. we ascended the Blue Ridge at Testna Gap, a dangerous drive as the pike was frozen over and snow everywhere; but not so steep as coming up the South side. On the very top I stopped to get some souveners of the Sublime Testna, then started down, face to the Sunny South, face towards home, dear old home. With all its faults there is no place like home. In going down the Mt. I met with the belled Razor back, a hog with a bell on was quite unusual to me. (they say some bell their children, I don't know about that, rather think they need to do so.)

Down the Mr. we stop at toll gate, where they charge passers going both ways, a buggy .25., pay toll and travel on mid the foothills in White Co. about 12m when night overtakes us and we get lodging at Mr. Allens. Allen, charges me .50 for feeding me & horse, & good bed. The old folks speek of the young and beautiful girl that I had seen at their house, wanting to go to Gainsville, I offer to carry her in my buggy; but the young folks say that one McGee has previously arranged to carry her to-morrow. (I hate that). I went through the Moonshine region the men are hospitable and kind. We go through Gainsville a nice city. In town we pass the home of Gen Longstreet, Lee's old warhorse.

At night we get to Mr. Simmon's home, where we find hospitality at its best. Two nice young ladies here, Misses Mannie & Fannie.

Jan. 6, To-day Mr. Hunnicutt and I bidding adieu to Mr. Simmons (He charges us nothing) In P.M. we pass through Duluth by Pittman and get to Norcross at Sundown. After taking supper at Toms I come on home, where I find them all well.

My expenses on trip was $2.30 I charge Tom $2.00 and expences for making the trip. The trip was interesting and instructing to me.

Jan. 7, A rainy day, I am glad to be at home.

Jan. 25, Cut pine & oak wood on T.B. pl. in A.M. In the P.M. at about 2 O'Clock while at home trying to split a small pine knot I struck a tree which knocked the axe down and cut my right great toe nearly off and a deep gash in the next toe. I did not feel the cut; but seeing the gash in my shoe I pulled shoe and sock off and saw my toe drop saw the marrow in

Nuggets of Nostalgia

the bone, the bone cut nicely into. I hopped to the house where my mother and little niece were, told them to get me some turpentine for I had cut my foot a little. Then told them I would have to get a doctor, and started Sally out to see if John was at home. John, my brother, not being at home, She soon came back, and I started her for my father who was hauling from T.B. place. Eliza, Johns wife came out, I told a negro teamster, Alf Bolton, to tell John who was in Norcross to send me a doctor. I put nothing on my toe but turpentine. My father and Mr. M.C. Jackson soon came. A negro woman also Mabry Jackson call in a few moments. About 1½ or 2 hours after cutting myself, the doctor came. Dr. Moses Richardson & Dr. Key. Dr. R. sewed two stiches on toe, this was, I believe, the worst pain I ever experienced, physically. He left me carbolic acid to put on toe. At night John Hamrick (my cousin) wife and 3 twin babies,—no one baby was, I believe, some older than the other two—came. (what a time). That night one baby would cry while the other two slept, then another would exercise, taking time about. With toe hurting and babies crying I did not sleep one wink the entire night.

Jan. 31, Toe doing well. I pass the time with my foot in a chair, while I read or work on Scrap Book.

Feb. 1, The bone in my toe is knitting back, a stinging crawling pain.

Feb. 29, Rain in early morning clearing up soon. Road workers meet to work road, but quit on account of mud. I go to Johns in A.M. Mr. Nelson Britt and 3rd wife spend the day. To-day is Mrs. Britt's birthday. She has only had 10 birthdays (40 yr. old) and will not have another till 8 more years. For a birthday dinner we set her down to a dish of Rutabaga Turnips which she seemed to relish, first thinking it was pumpkin.

Sept. 25, My birthday I am to-day 25 years old. I am in good health, out of prison, and am enjoying many other undeserved blessings from the hand of God.

Dec. 17, Oliver and myself go to Atlanta. After getting to Atlanta we go to J.W. Powells and to my Brothers W.R. Ray's where I leave Oliver, and then I go to Hell and meet Hela goddess of the Furies. How sad that one enjoying the richest of blessings from the bountiful hand of the true and merciful giver of all good—the eternal God,—should do as I do this P.M.

But God followed me even there—His mercy is past finding out, its extent to erring mortal.

Dec. 18, After trading some we start for home. Windy and cool.

To-day with Hells mantle about me I am reminded of the unchangeable God. When about ten or eleven years old I one day ask God that I might

never see a certain neighbor boy again on earth; because this boy prevented me from going to church that day. And on to-day I hear of his death and I never saw him from that day that I prayed to see him no-more.
Dec. 19, In torment. At night my reason seems about to leave me, I get up from my seat and walk.
Dec. 20, In torment. I go to Bethel in A.M. and P.M.
Dec. 21, In torment. I go to Norcross in A.M. I now understand my condition. I have been looking death in the face for the past few days. Father builds garden.
Dec. 22, The light breaks into my darkness some. Father finishes building the garden.
Dec. 31, And to-day ends the year of our Lord 1896. An eventful year to me, starting out with a trip into the mountain country of North Georgia—a wild picturesque journey across the Blue Ridge. Then an accident, cut my toe off, which kept me quiet for a month. Then a little love breeze which amounted to nothing.

Learned from experience in 1896 that it is best to—

Handle an axe with care, and not be cutting wood at root of a tree.
Not braggingly defy the Devil; for he has great power and can control the will of man—causing him to do things he would not—when permitted by God. Always seek the protection of God from temptation and power of the devil.

That the 3rd Sunday of April is to me an unlucky day, on that day my evil genius rules, and I had better, in the future, lock myself in my room and get some one to tie me to the bed post
Always wait till ground drys before plowing it.
Good-bye 1896

No journal was found for 1897.

1898

January 1, 1898 New Years Holiday. I pray God's blessings to be upon me and my home this year; may he be our God, our protector, our director in all things, our constant companion.

I buy this book to-day.
Jan. 17, My horse, Maudie, is very sick, we send for Mr. Davenport to help us give her some medicine.

Marion scribbled a dedication to the war between the United States and Spain on this 1898 journal cover. *Courtesy of Clifton Ray.*

Jan. 17, continued, My mare suffers great pain all day and dies about 8 O'Clock P.M.

Just one month ago, Dec. 16, I bought her in Atlanta for $33.00. She was I thought just my ideal of a horse in every particular—a real beauty and true to work anywhere, very sensible. We did not understand her sickness that resulted in her death. It seems to be at this time a heavy loss to me, but God knows what is best. "The Lord gave and the Lord hath taken away, blessed be the name of the Lord."

Jan. 31, I plow in P.M. A drunken man comes by the house in A.M. Lilly threatens to burst his skull with fire stick whereupon he leaves.

Feb. 16, Very cool. Our battleship Maine *destroyed last night at Havanna. Maine—256 lives lost—in Havanna harbor on the night of the 18th inst. Supposed to be the work of Spanish treachery. It may mean war.*

Remembering Norcross

March 1, I work on road, Peachtree, in A.M., plow in oats in P.M.
March 9, The war clouds continue to gather, the booming of cannon in Atlanta tells us that war is coming.
April 1, All fools day.
Apr. 10, Sunday. This is Easter Sunday. I ate seven eggs at breakfast.
   Congress enact declaration of war.
   Three cheers for the red, white and blue.
Apr. 27, Rain again last night.
   War was formally declared to be existing between United States and Spain The Stars and Stripes now wave over the Philippines.
May 8, Sunday, U.S. soldiers are now in Cuba.
May 12, Over 300 cars of soldiers passed through Atlanta last night and to-day enroute to the Southern sea cost preparatory to invasion.
May 21, Father helps dig grave for Mr. Raineys infant (one week old) at Old Harmony.
May 24, Bed up potato ground in A.M. An Evil day A Spanish fleet of 4 powerful battleships and 3 swift torpedo boats destroyers have outwitted the two American squadrons. All war news is now under rigid censorship, and we do not hear the bad part. No news of future movements of troops or of ships is allowed.
July 1, I plow cotton. Very, very dry. Lieut. Col. Theodore Roosevelt's Rough Riders fight against the Spanish
July 3, Sunday, The Yankee cavalry now in Cuba is very low with yellow fever, in camp.
July 4, America's Birthday.
July 18, Santiago (of Cuba) has surrendered yesterday at 9 O'Clock. The town bands played; "Star Spangled Banner," "Rally 'Round the Flag Boys" and "The Stars and Stripes Forever."
Aug. 24, The record of August is not correct in every particular owing to my sickness. Turner stayed with us nine nights while I was sick. Chas. Young calls in P.M. warns me to work road Saturday.
   Manilla, Phillippines, surrendered to Gen. Merritt and Admiral Dewey on Aug. 13. Only 5 Americans killed. 7000 Spanish prisoners taken. Lieut. Brumby, of flagship Olympia, *a native Georgian, hoisted the stars and stripes over Manilla. A peace protocol has been signed between U.S. and Spain. M. Cambou French minister at Washington acting for Spain. Spain agrees to evacuate Cuba and relinquish all claims or jurisdictions over the island; to cede the island of Porto Rico and all other Spanish isles in Antilles to the United States. The fate of Phillippines to be decided later on. A Commission from both countries will meet in Paris in Oct. to arrange*

treaty. Hostilities between U.S. and Spain have ceased. Cervera and all other Spanish held prisoners in U.S. are being given their liberty. Yellow fever at Key West.

Aug. 25, I slowly improve. Lilly, Jodie and Oliver go with wheat to mill at Norcross, they also go to Cemetery to clean off Bro. Joe's grave.

Sept. 22, Thunder showers. I pick cotton. Father carries Lilly to Norcross in A.M. to have teeth pulled.

    Dave Dean and Will Nesbitt is yet in camp at Griffin. A Johns boy of Norcross is also in Army, I do not know regiment.

Oct. 15, Jack Frost's first visit.

Dec. 26, All our family except Oliver and all of Bro Tom's family except Walter, take dinner with Bro. John. Cool and windy. Fitzhugh Lee is governor general of the province of Havannah, Cuba. Total Eclipse of Moon 6 to 9 o'clock P.M.

1899

Jan. 6, 1899, A rainy day. Father stays with Mr. Gullege who is very low, Turner stayed with him last night.

Jan. 7, Cold. I go to Norcross to get School books in A.M. Jodie is some better.

Jan. 11, Rainy. Pigs got out of pen last night, but was easily caught.

Feb. 4, I go to mill in A.M. and at noon. Mule sick, Davenport bleeds mule in P.M. cording neck with loop and bow knot and cutting on side of rope next to head.

Feb. 5, Sunday. We give sick mule dose of lard and Assofoeida and nuxvornica, mule is better in P.M. Bro. John calls in P.M. also Prof. Hicks, Bijah Nuckolls. Mr. Davenport and others call to see mule in P.M.

Feb. 12, It snows! it snows! about 6 inches falls to-day.

Feb. 13, Cold Monday. The thermometer registers at nine (9) degrees below zero. The coldest weather in many years, the North wind has blowed a terrific gale all day, drifting up the snow in places to a depth of 5 and 6 feet leaving the ground bare in other places. Awful cold, coldest weather since the cold Friday and Saturday Feb. 7 and 8, 1835.

Record of the mercury at Georgia points last Monday, Feb. 13—Cold Monday.

Atlanta=8 below zero

Rome=7 below zero

Notations on the 1899 diary cover record one of the coldest days in Georgia history, February 13. *Courtesy of Clifton Ray.*

Nuggets of Nostalgia

Carrollton=15 below zero
Marietta=8 below zero
Athens=12 below zero
Lawrenceville=9 below zero
Norcross=9 below zero

Mar. 2, Mrs. W.H. Gulledge died this A.M. at 6 O'Clock,—Consumption. Father goes to Norcross and to assist where the corpse is.
Mar. 21, Haul manure Hugh Ray was bit by a rabid dog (mad-dog) yesterday, Dr. Dicken's cauterized the wound with caustic

Apr. 8, Cold wind and showery (some hail) from North west. Snow was from 4 to 6 inches in states of Va., N.C. and South Carolina. We haul guano in A.M. we have got one ton (10 sacks) of Owl Brand from Martin & Johnson for which we promise 325 lbs cotton. I scour house in A.M. Walter Ray takes dinner with us. Lilly has made arrangements to work in Atlanta
On 10th day of April 1899 Lillie went to Atlanta to work and this troubled me, I asked God what to do, the answer was "Seek the one that has fled." I then commenced to write to Lillie. I oftened asked to be directed, I was told to "Strengthen her," to love her, and that though trouble might come yet she was my companion.
On the 21st day of May 1899, we were to-gether at Bethlehem Church.
On the 18th day of June, 3rd Sunday, I asked her to be my wife.
July 4, Independence Day.
July 17, I meet Lily at carshed in A.M. she goes to C.H. C's at Howell's Station. I come home on belle train at night.
    Our correspondence continued and Lillie gave me the promise to share the joys and burdens of life with me in a letter I received on July 28th 1899.
August 1, Crops are looking very fine now. I carry 20 melons to town=1.05.
Aug. 5, Day of work on old Harmony Grave yard.
Aug. 6, Sunday. I go to Bro. Johns in P.M. Cora and Claudia Holbrook stay all day with Sallie, Bro. Tom, Mattie and Annie call in P.M.
Aug. 7, I carry 22 melons to town get .90c. Lillie and Jodie return home on belle train from Chas. Cunningham.
Aug. 8, We finish hoeing rutabagas. <u>Very Dry</u>.
Aug. 15, Eugene Kranser, the Bavarian, puts rock wall in our well, we have Tom Ware to help us draw water and let down rock. Cloudy, sprinkle.
Aug. 17, I pick peas in A.M. Father plows in new ground. The Supreme

Remembering Norcross

Court of France is now on the revision trial—second trial—of Capt. Dreyfus Jews and Anti Jews are rioting. Dreyfus's chief counsel was shot on his way to court. Another French revolution imminent.

Aug. 26, I carry 18 small melons, 1 pk. beans and 2 doz eggs to Norcross. I get .85 for load.

Aug. 27, Sunday. I go to Bethel. Cloudy, rain at night. Three Norcross boys have gone to fight the Fillipinos, Ira Haney, Arnold Ivester, Carl Wooten.

Sept. 17, Sunday Mr. P.B. Starnes store was robbed last night of $50 or $60 worth.

Sept. 25, My birthday I am 28 years old. We pick cotton in A.M.

Sept. 27, Jack Frost's first visit, very cool. Dewey arrives in New York.

Sept. 28, We sell first bale cotton, 690. Dewey lands at New York.

Sept. 29, Dewey Day in New York City.

Nov. 9, We finish sowing wheat. We haul 5th bale to gin.

Nov. 10, I go to gin for seed in A.M. I am taken with "ketch" in my back cannot move myself without great pain.

Nov. 11, I am some better. I get last antenuptial letter from Lillie, I inform father of our marriage.

Nov. 12, Sunday. I am able to walk up to Hoyle P.O. in P.M. Father and Oliver go to church. I write my last antenuptial letter to Lillie.

Nov. 13, I haul corn. I go to Rev. J.H. Cooks at noon to get him to officiate at my marriage, I do not find him home, so I decide that he is not the man. Warm.

Nov. 14, We finish hauling up corn in A.M. We make 52 large one horse (5 bu.) loads. About 260 bus. I pick cotton in P.M. I prepare to go to my wedding to-morrow. Rain at night. I will now give my main reasons for marrying my brother's widdow, as I aim to marry Lillie on to-morrow.

   I love Lillie.

   I believe it is Gods purpose for me to marry Lillie, why I believe so is because of the following evidences;—A short time after my brother died it came into my mind that I must marry Lillie, it caused me to tremble and I commenced to fight the very thought of so doing. When in trouble, and when I do not know which way to go I have often asked God to direct me, I would take up a Bible close my eyes ask God to direct me open the Bible put my finger upon the page and in the verse that my finger rested upon I would find an answer to the question I had asked.

   On the 14th of March 1897, Lillie and Jodie came to our house to live. I asked God should I act towards Lillie as a brother to a sister, the answer was "Love them to the end." I said I could not be to her more than a brother the answer was, "It is the work of God."

46

Nuggets of Nostalgia

Strive as I would to put the thought of her aside, I could not, She alone was ever in my thoughts.

At Noon 1st day of May 1898 I looked in the well, Sunlight reflected by glass, I saw her form there.

So I go to marry Lillie believing it is the pleasure of God.

Nov. 15, 1899 My Wedding Day. I leave home at Sun up it is a very foggy morning and the Belle train does not see me at Buchannan's crossing in time to stop at right place, but runs on nearly out of sight. I think I am left but the train comes back after me. When I get to Atlanta I go at once and engage the services of Rev. D.M. Mathews to marry me. I buy suit of clothes for $8.00 tie, cuff etc, .75 Pills, Medacamentum=.25.

I buy license of ordinary Hulsey for 1.75, the clerk makes a mistake in name so I go back to office and have Ordinary to give new license.

I go to State Capitol and listen to house and Senate of Georgia Legislature. At 2:40 O'Clock P.M. I am married to Lillie

At Howells Station. Lillie and I with Jodie and Vada go to Waterworks in P.M.

Nov. 17, I go up on train with trunk to carshed meet Lillie, Jodie and Vada at shed, in town rest of day, see Bro. Randolph on street. We come home at night on Belle train. God has been with me.

Dec. 25, Christmas Day. At home most of day. I go to put presents on Christmas tree at Bethel Church. Lillie and I get two nice apples.

Goodbye 1899—The nineteenth century and the year of 1900 will soon be forever gone, and "We all within our graves shall sleep, A hundred years to come."

1900

January, 1900 I have been married two months.

Feb. 22, Washington's Birthday. Very Cold. Albert (Jake) Warbington dies at 10 O'Clock, my father is by his bedside when he dies. He died of Consumption.

May 28, Total eclipse of the Sun, line of totality fifty five miles wide passing from New Orleans, La. to Norfolk, Va. The magnitude of the eclipse here was 0.963, the suns diameter being 1. The U.S. Naval Observatory taken photographs and made observations of eclipse at Barnesville Ga. Strange shadowy lines appeared around the Western and Southern horizon, the darkness quickly gathered, and a gloom seemed over the earth. Darkest period lasted one and one fourth (1 1/4) minutes.

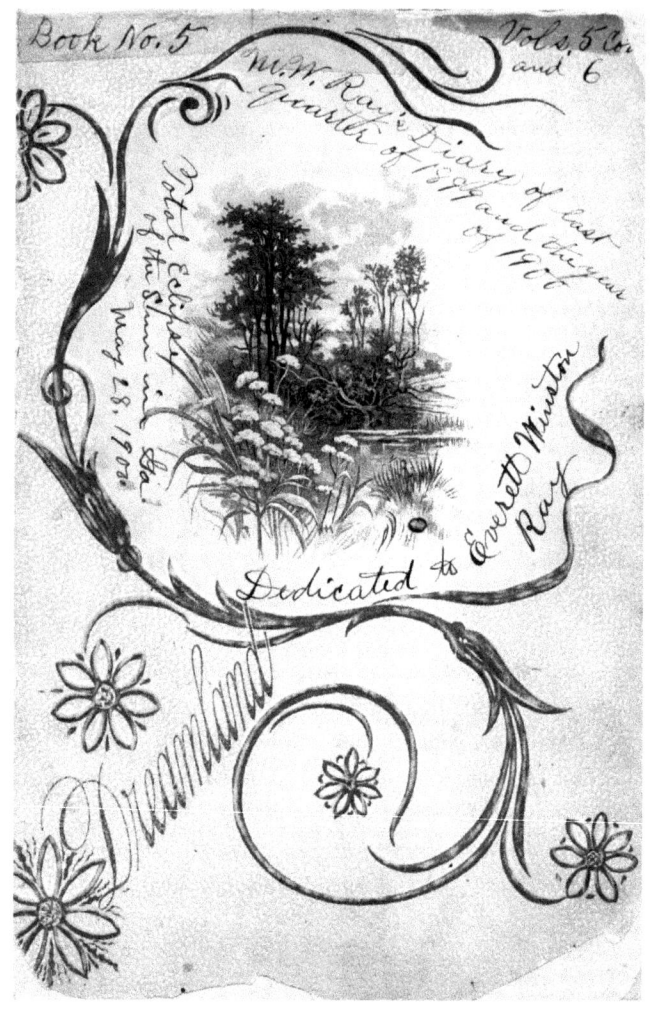

The birth of Marion and Lillie Ray's son, Everett Winston, is marked on the 1900 diary cover. *Courtesy of Clifton Ray.*

June 26, I was very sick last night. Rainy. War has commenced between China and the rest of the world. The Chinese secret society, Boxers, have set out to kill all foreigners.

July 2, Plow corn, rain at night. The allied forces silenced Chinese forts and entered Tien Tesin June 30. Americans and British were first to enter.

July 4, Nations Birthday. We find first cotton bloom.

Sept. 16, We all, except Mama and Lillie, go to Bethlehem sermon by Rev. J.H. Cook, subject Gods love.

Galveston Horror.

Galveston, Texas was destroyed by a storm on Sept. 9th. Five (5000) thousand people were killed and $20000000 dollars of property destroyed.

Nuggets of Nostalgia

Oct. 22, Our boy Everett Winston Ray is borned between two and three O'Clock in A.M.

I have to start two miles for doctor afoot, but good Mr. Bob Brewer furnishes me with a mule and I get Dr. M. Richardson at our house in an hour from the time I start. Father fetches Mrs. Lark Young and Mrs. J.H. Cook.

The baby weighed nine pounds net or ten pounds with clothes.

May God keep and direct our Everett.

A cloudy rainy day.

Nov. 6, National election. I go to Norcross in A.M. Pay Dr. Richardson $6.00 for his visit Oct. 22. I have my hair cut. I vote the democrat ticket—Bryan for president, Stevenson for vice president.

Nov. 7, First frost. William McKinley was elected Pres. of U.S. Yesterday. Theodore Roosevelt Vice Pres.

Dec. 22, 1900, Everett Winston Ray is two months old.

Dec. 24, Christmas Eve, Mr. Will Stanley, wife and four (4) children stay with us to-night, Santa Claus must fill six stockings, 4 Stanleys, Jodie's and Everett's.

Dec. 25, Christmas Day. A bright and beautiful day. The last Christmas of the nineteenth century. I stay at home.

1901

Dedicated to the Twentieth Century and Electric Advancement.

*Messages sent by
Marconi and received
across Atlantic Ocean
by Ether waves without
wires in December*

January 1, 1901. 7:30 A.M. The new year of 1901 and the new century—twentieth century is here. I was awake last night at midnight and saw the end of the old year 1900 and the end of the nineteenth century, and saw the beginning of 1901 and the beginning of the twentieth Century.

Mch. 20, Rain in A.M. I make trap to catch hawk that kills our hens. I make a bee hive.

Mch. 22, Everett Winston Ray is five months old. We catch hawk in trap and have hawk for dinner, first I ever ate of, it was nearly as good as chicken.

In 1901, Marion noted the electronic advancement of messages sent across the ocean over airwaves by Guglielmo Marconi. *Courtesy of Clifton Ray.*

May 30, Confederate Veterans are in session at Memphis.
Aug. 23, We sell melons, beans & potatoes in Norcross $2.05. I pick beans in P.M.
Aug. 24, I sell beans, melons and peaches at Norcross. I have bad luck to get my wagon shaft broke, cost me .75.
Aug. 28 Rev. Green Henderson was drowned in Etowah river while crossing on a flat last Sunday, 25 inst. He was going to his church. He was found to-day. Rev. Green Henderson was an old friend.
Sept. 25, My birthday, I am thirty.
Oct. 22, Everett Winston Ray is one year old. I pick cotton and haul corn.
Nov. 17, Sunday. Some great phenomena have transpired in the heavens the past week, on the 14th the earth was in the path of the Leonid Meteiors, I

Nuggets of Nostalgia

saw some shooting in the heavens—about two a minute from the constellation Leo. On the 15th the Moon was in conjunction with Venus, Jupiter, and Saturn, the conjunction of the Moon with three planets on one day does not occur but once in three or four hundred years. Venus will pass Jupiter on the 18th and Saturn on the 19th.
Nov. 18, We gather corn.
Nov. 19, It snows, it snows, for six hours a heavy snow storm rages, but the snow soon melts away. The earliest snow fall in Ga. since 1882.

No journal was found for 1902. Marion and Lillie had a daughter, Lola, in this year.

1903

Jan. 22, 1903 Lola Eunice Edna is seven months old. I plow. Mrs. Bagwell is killed by train to-day, she attempted to cross track when train was too near by, I sit up at Mr. Harpers part of the night with the corpse.
Jan. 23, I plow, warm.
March 21, I go to mill in A.M. Rainy. I sell 65 cents worth of seed potatoes.
March 22, Lola Eunice Edna Ray is nine months old
Aug. 6, I sow rutabagas. Lillie and Aunt Adlissa cook and prepare for soldiers reunion at Norcross on tomorrow. First ripe watermelon.
Aug. 7, We all attend the old soldiers reunion at Norcross, Camp L.P. Thomas No. 1476.
Nov. 25, Rainy, haul wood in P.M.
Nov. 26, Thanksgiving Day. I have much to be thankful for, we have all been spaired through the year to the present. Out of debt and have something to eat.
Dec. 1, Lillie is not well.
Dec. 3, Our little angel baby is borned and goes to God to-day at about 11:30 o-clock A.M. We named it Ollive Angelina. This has been an awful day for us, but the mercy of God spaired the life of the mother—the little babe rests in peace.
Dec. 4, Father attends to getting coffin and buying lot in cemetery at Norcross.
Dec. 5, After funeral service we carry our little babe Ollive Angelina and put it away in the grave in the cemetery at Norcross, lot #184. Eula Ray and Bruna Nash spend the night with us.

Dec. 6, Lillie's Mother came last night to stay with us a few days.
Dec. 11, Lillie slowly improves.
Dec. 12, I go to Norcross in A.M., I get receipt for cemetery lots Nos. 184, 185, 1/2 186
    10 X 25 ft. I pay for them $5.00. I sell 2 bus. ruta-bagas=1.20. I pick cotton in P.M.
Dec. 13, Sunday. At home. Bro. Tom & Mattie call in P.M. Rain last night, cool to-day.
Dec. 21, We cut wood—our Christmas wood. Jodie returns home in P.M.
Dec. 22, Scour in A.M., haul wood in P.M. Father stays all day at Norcross.
Dec. 23, I go to Norcross in A.M., haul wood in P.M.
Dec. 24, Christmas Eve. Bro. Tom, Eula and Annie call in A.M. they bring Jodie a toy piano, Everett a train, and Lola a dog; they bring Mother a cape, father some socks, Aunt Adlissa some stockings and Lillie some Towels all Christmas presents.
Dec. 25, Christmas Day. At home. Santa Claus brings Jodie fancy cup and sauser, harp, coconut, orange, banana, apple, candy; he brings Everett silver knife and fork, harp, banana, orange, apple, candies and a toy watch; he brings Lola a doll, orange, banana, apple and candies.
Dec. 31, I help Father and Mr. Craten Green put up wire fence around Old Harmony Cemetery.

The old year will soon be gone forever, it brought us many sorrows and some pleasures. God has blessed us in many ways. Our greatest sorrow was the giving up of our little infant girl, Ollive Angelina, who was borned and died Dec. 3, 1903, and was burried Dec. 5 in Norcross Cemetery Lot No. 184

No journal was found for 1904. The last journal found was written only in the month of January.

1905

Jan. 1, 1905 New-Years day. Sunday. Jan. 15, Sunday, cold. Mother tells me that she does not believe that she can live much longer.
Jan. 17, Mother takes her bed.
Jan. 18, 19, We think at night that mother is about gone.

Nuggets of Nostalgia

Jan. 19, Mother's Birthday she is seventy nine years old.
June 20, Mother is very low, we tellephone for Bros. Tom and Dock also Aunt Adlissa and Sallie Turner, they all come.
Jan. 21, Mother is very low she tells me as she has many times before that she is ready to go that all is well with her, she asks me to look after Father also hopes that she and I may meet in heaven.
Jan. 22, Sunday. Our neighbors are continually with us in our great trouble.
Jan. 26, Very cold. Mother tells Everett and Lola good-night and asks God to bless them should she not live through the night.
   It is an awful night for us.
Jan. 27, May God help me, My darling Mother passes into eternity to rest in peace with her Lord and Saviour and enter into that glory reserved in heaven for her.
   She dies between eleven and twelve O'Clock,
   My dearest love is gone.
   God help me just before she died she embraced me and told me she would soon leave me.
Jan. 27, I buy coffin for Mother=$40.00.
Jan. 28, Sunday. We put away in the tomb the body of my sainted Mother, amid the many relatives, neighbors and friends, in Old Harmony Cemetery.
   The funeral was conducted by Elders J.H. Cook and Jas. Livesy who spoke of how she understood her salvation to be secured to her by the love and grace of God through Jesus her redeemer.

   Her faith in her Lord and Saviour sustained her through the many dark trials of her life of 79 years and 8 days.
   The giving up of my Mother is the greatest trial of my life, but I know that she is in heaven, and may I be carried there.

Strive On
Many have reached
The top of the ladder of fame,
Then why not you!
Many have left
On the pages of time a name,
Then why not you!
Have ever a goal
That is just ahead in the lane,

Remembering Norcross

With the passing of his mother in 1905, Marion brought his journal writing to a close. *Courtesy of Clifton Ray.*

Strive on and on.
Have ever an aim
That is fixed on a higher plane,
Strive on and on.

A Poem by M.W. Ray

Marion Wesley Ray was born September 25, 1871, near Norcross, in Gwinnett County, Georgia. He departed this life April, 2, 1944, at the age of seventy-five and a half years. His daughter Lola wrote a poem eulogizing her father, which was found tucked in the 1903 edition.

By 1906, Tom Ray, son of T.B. Ray depicted in the diaries, had become a prominent citizen of Norcross and was president of the Southern Harness and Leather Company. Tom moved his family's original farmhouse,

Nuggets of Nostalgia

eventually attaching it to another small home, which stands as one home today. He built a charming two-story home on family farmland east of the newly named dirt road North Peachtree Street. Built for entertaining and raising his family, the larger house was the setting for many parties hosted by his daughters as they grew up. Noye Nesbit, a talented early craftsman, hand-crafted each mantel for the six original fireplaces, a few remain in the home. A large open area upstairs was a gathering place for the family, who played billiards while Mrs. Ray sat in the upper front bay window to sew.

Tom Ray operated the first dairy in Norcross, maintaining a number of cows in his backyard between his home, the property of Gus McDaniel and the railroad tracks. He utilized several buildings as milking barns and made local deliveries in a Model T Ford pickup truck.

The milk was prepared in glass quart bottles with pasteboard stoppers. The daily deliveries were vital, since many homes had no refrigeration before World War II. Most folks stored the milk in buckets lowered to the cool depths of their wells, often spilling some milk out and forcing them to flush the well for purity of the water. Customers were encouraged to return the stoppers so Ray could wash them and reuse them. This process was not likely a sanitary operation.

Built in 1910 by Tom Ray, this home was the site of many parties, and Ray also operated the first dairy in town from here. *Courtesy of Clifton Ray.*

Remembering Norcross

In 1937, the house was purchased from Annie Ray, a daughter of Tom, by Dr. W.W. Puett who had a medical office upstairs in the Kent building on Jones Street. He eventually saw patients at the home. If the stoic black walnut tree and two grand magnolias, planted well before 1865, could, they would whisper of simpler days gone by.

Holy Row

The earliest Christian congregation gathering closest to the rapidly growing town of Norcross was Medlock Chapel, which is believed to have come together around 1818. Half-buried tombstones in the early churchyard bear names of settlers such as Martha Hoyle, who died in 1831, and Allen Jones, who passed in 1838. A second church, Flint Hill, began drawing great crowds to rousing revivals and camp meetings it hosted between 1825 and 1862. A regiment of volunteers, known as the Flint Hill Grays, was outfitted by ladies of the church during the War Between the States.

Reconstruction brought new cities needing new plans. Communities grow when residents have a place to shop, work and pray. "Cousin John" Thrasher laid out several streets for Norcross during the boom year of 1870. On Church Street, just north of the depot, Thrasher set aside five four-acre lots, on which he built houses and promptly offered them to five traveling preachers. Although officially named Church Street, the dirt path was affectionately known as "Holy Row."

A single meeting building was built on Holy Row the same year, with an intended use as a schoolhouse on Mondays through Fridays, a place for Masonic lodge meetings on Saturdays and a place for a variety of Christian denominations to sing out in praise each Sunday morning.

Several denominations were represented, each having a part-time preacher who would hold service for his flock once a month in Norcross and then travel the countryside of a growing Gwinnett. The nomadic preachers followed a path along either the Lawrenceville or the Tucker and Duluth "circuits," visiting rural areas to preach on each of the other three Sundays in any given month. Each denomination took turns leading the Norcross services. Townspeople attended every Sunday, just with a different preacher.

Remembering Norcross

Established in 1875 as Flint Hill Methodist Church, later renamed First United Methodist of Norcross, this building was refurbished for use as a meeting hall. *Courtesy of Evelyn Norman.*

The situation of sharing preachers created an unusual but very friendly atmosphere of fellowship among attendees.

Attendees of the new church of Norcross, which was pretty much everyone, gathered to listen to the Methodist, Baptist or Presbyterian preachers. Those who remember hearing the stories from those who attended church in this unusual manner say it inspired "such a good feeling" of fellowship in the community.

On May 17, 1872, seventeen people met to begin a separate Baptist congregation. As the Baptists began building their own church building across from the city park, Jonathan Norcross donated a bell for the tower. Norcross First Baptist later moved to property that the Wino family farmed just a short walk north along North Peachtree Street.

About 1871, the Flint Hill Methodist group, meeting on Holy Row, formed plans to build in town. By 1875, construction of Norcross First Methodist, financed by businessmen in town, was completed. In 1896, Miss Lola Key began teaching a Sunday school class she dubbed the "Golden Key." Over the decades, attendance soared, forcing the congregation to a newer location along Beaver Ruin Road, where it celebrated 189 years of services on April 24, 2009. The original church building, gently restored, is now a community meeting place and theatre.

Each era of strife banded residents together in benevolent Christian sentiment. Martha Ruth Simpson and her twin sister Sue were born sickly and small one cold January day in 1919. Young parents Ollie and Anne Mclure Simpson were overwhelmed with the task of nursing strength into both mother and babes. Their wood framed house was warmed by only a fireplace in one small back room. Norcross neighbors willingly increased their own daily chores to keep the young family's fire stoked with extra wood that they split and carried by.

Nuggets of Nostalgia

This church building, built in 1899, housed the first Presbyterian congregation of Norcross. *Author's collection.*

Martha and Sue Simpson play happily in their yard. *Courtesy of the Nesbit family.*

Folks remember a preacher once asking Ollie, known to all as a crackup character, "Don't you think you owe the Lord a little something?" Ollie jibed back, "Yes, but the Lord's not pushing me like the others do!"

Atlanta's Favorite Summer Resort

Hot and weary Atlanta dwellers escaped the dust of the city by catching a four-coach commuter train known as the Airline Belle, which ran daily out to Norcross at 8:00 a.m. and shifted into reverse for the return trip at 6:00 p.m. Salesmen rode out to fill the shelves of the four general stores, traveling teachers arrived in time to ring the school bell each morning and the rich elite of Atlanta departed the Belle in Norcross for a weekend holiday.

Before the extension of the rails northward to Duluth, Gainesville and eventually Washington, D.C., Norcross was popular as a summer resort offering cool, lakeside camping within city limits or more civilized accommodations for the wealthy at one of three popular hotels in town. Both the two-story Medlock and the impressive three-floor and twenty-nine-room Brunswick hotels were built along Thrasher Street in the town's boom year of 1866. The Martin Hotel sprang up soon after on the opposite side of the tracks, just east of the depot and its developing rail lines.

Merchants riding out from Atlanta offered their wares from stores along Main Street and inside one of the display rooms of each hotel. Local farmers offered fresh produce overflowing from baskets in the flats of their wagons. The Brunswick was well kept in the winter by Captain Webb and in the summer by Captain Holbrook. You could dine on real butter—without the features of Oleomargarine—fat yellow-legged chicken and mutton from the mountainsides, all served on clean linen tablecloths. A group of Norcross businessmen worked out sort of a guarantee with the railroad. The group proposed reimbursement to the railroad if the commuter whistle stop venture was not profitable. Between the large display rooms offered to "drummers" selling their wares and the livery renting horse and wagon for

Remembering Norcross

The Medlock Hotel was one of three popular resort locations when Norcross boomed with tourists and businessmen. *Courtesy of Evelyn Norman.*

salesmen wishing to peddle throughout the countryside, the venture proved successful. It was so lucrative, in fact, that those guarantors were released from any obligation.

Many festive diversions were planned for Dodson Park, renamed Thrasher Park in 1934, with merchants cleverly setting aside Tuesday and Friday evenings for rousing band performances under the park's pavilion. A trill of notes lofting from the popular city park richly embodied the spirit of Norcross. Folks staying at the Brunswick, the Medlock or the Martin danced with gussied-up locals on dirt streets, smoothed over by a layer of cornmeal, to a brass beat.

A boisterous atmosphere emanated from Norcross's bustling train stop, soon promoted as "Atlanta's Favorite Summer Resort." Wives on holiday would dress for an afternoon stroll across the tracks, meeting their husbands, who traveled back from their business in Atlanta. Norcross residents walked up to town just to watch other folks' comings and goings. A social elitism crept in on Norcross as the visiting ladies appeared, to locals, to be "puttin' on airs" by donning the lorgnette, a set of eye spectacles that plain folk called "eyeglasses on a stick."

When the Richmond-Danville line expanded northward, passengers and commerce began traveling to Duluth, Gainesville and Tocooa.

Nuggets of Nostalgia

Martha Simpson Nesbit recalls boarding the rails with her twin sister for a big trip to Gainesville.

Daddy [Ollie] would load my sister Sue and I up to visit our aunt who lived in Gainesville. It was quite a big trip for us since we usually just went down to the depot twice a week to watch folks coming in and going out.

We rode up through Duluth then on to Gainesville. Our aunt didn't have any children of her own so she really made a commotion about us riding up there to visit with her.

Martha recalls how impressive the Brunswick was to her as a young girl:

It had three stories, with wide porches along the fronts of the first and second floors. Both porch fronts ran along the streets so everyone could see all the guests settin' out in rockers, just taking in the lush trees of the city park. We would all dress up a little bit just to walk downtown because Sue and I liked seeing the traveling teachers who came for a stay there.

The once brilliant Brunswick Hotel was converted to apartments at the end of World War II, when the train no longer made a stop in Norcross. The striking building, soaring to an amazing three stories, was demolished to make way for a new post office.

Even before the rich elite discovered the resort hotels of Norcross, the area was a popular camping spot. On long, hot summer days, swimmers dipped in Hopkins Mill Pond or cooled their toes in a little lake that once graced property that is now the backyards of new homes on Lake Drive. During the Civil War, Southern units pitched tents along the banks of the little lake seeking rest. Confederate veterans' groups returned to camp there for postwar reunions. Large shade trees, some still standing, lined the grassy green banks of the cool, spring-fed lake, now no more than a trickle of a creek.

"My grandfather told me about the soldiers camping around the lake," Bob Warbington recalls, pointing to an earthen dam still visible on the lower portion of his family's land. "I don't remember ever hearing why it was drained. I know my grandfather built the stone-walled pool back in the '30s, replenishing its water each summer from the natural spring" that gurgles into the small creek. Hearty swimmers ignored the frogs and some snakes that also enjoyed the pool.

Before enrolling at Georgia Technical Institute, Worley Adams, at the request of his parents, earned some extra cash by helping dig the eight-foot-deep rectangular pool.

Remembering Norcross

Confederate soldiers often held reunions in Norcross. These were likely members of the Flint Hill Grays, a volunteer regiment. *Courtesy of Evelyn Norman.*

Lillian Webb fondly recalls a summer memory of her childhood: "Bertha 'Grandma' Warbington, would sit down there by the pool in a old wooden chair collecting ten cents from us children who walked over there for a swim. In those days there were two bathhouses and I remember lying out on blankets under the hardwood trees to eat a sandwich as we would swim all day." As an adult, Lillian served several terms as mayor of Norcross.

Two wooden bathhouses, the serene lake and Grandma Warbington are gone, leaving only a trickling creek and vague ruin outline remains of the first stone and mortar dirt-walled pool in Gwinnett County, Georgia. A garden grows over the once popular summer site where folks would pay a dime to swim all day.

Apple Pie, Baseball and Norcross

First played by Civil War soldiers as a distraction between skirmishes, "rounders" was nurtured from pickup players kicking dust around an open lot to professional players, scouted, drafted and paid a pretty penny, to the game we know as baseball, eventually played for stadiums full of ticket-purchasing fans.

Both Union and Confederate companies broke ranks to enjoy a pickup game, using bottle caps or knotted rags as balls and sticks or stiff leather straps as bats. Often the time spent playing a "bat ball game" was the only cheerful part of an otherwise disturbing era in American history, and as a result, soldiers noted the game when writing home. In many letters, enlisted men describe the game becoming a "mania" at camp, playing while "musketry could be heard in the distance."

At the end of the War Between the States, the game, with an ever-modifying set of rules and equipment like leather gloves and wooden bats, came home with the soldiers. The sport of smacking down a hard or "dead" ball, rounding three bases and scoring at home, while your opponent tries to trick a "striker" into whiffing his "club" without striking the ball, therefore striking the striker out or tagging a runner, earning a total of three outs per inning, spread east to west, from state to state. Amateur clubs, colleges and towns formed teams whose games gained spectator popularity for the most part because, with no electricity or modern forms of entertainment, there just wasn't anything else for folks to do but play or watch "town ball."

Teams began traveling to compete with one another at highly promoted exhibition games, and baseball migrated across the newly re-United States. Players were advertised as amateurs, even though admission was charged at the gate. Newspaper reporters uncovered that players' compensation was

Remembering Norcross

Shown from left to right are Hugh Twitty, Verb Eason, Blount Burchelle, Los Terell, Frank "Poo Doo" Robertson, Carl Garner, Ollie Simpson and Garland Terrell. They were all players for the 1910 Norcross Baseball Club. *Courtesy of the Norcross Old Timers Baseball Association.*

more than a cracker or cake, as was the fashion for many who played on teams sponsored by the National Biscuit Company.

By 1869, the Cincinnati Red Stockings became the first professional team formed by scouting, drafting and paying players who boasted a big bat, quick feet or a strong arm, which equaled great crowd appeal. The Red Stockings first opposed "town teams," eventually competing with other newly forming teams, building stadiums full of seats in the cities of New York, Boston and Chicago.

In 1911, the "dead ball," a hard ball allowing only grounders and bunts, was replaced with a cork-cored leather-stitched ball that players discovered they could loft over an infielder's head, past the centerfield fences and sometimes out of the new stadiums, rich with green grass and red brick dust pitching mounds, rising up in cities from East Coast to West.

After forty years of low batting averages, the new ball, with a great propensity to sail, launched the popularity of baseball into the stratosphere. Word spread through the newspapers of home run hitters and sky-high fly balls caught by men with quick reactions and great glove handling, drawing great numbers of ticket-purchasing fans.

Nuggets of Nostalgia

With the onslaught of radio broadcasts, young men, imagining the game in black-and-white as they listened, started to believe that they could hone their skills in hitting or catching to cash in on signing bonuses and salaries that professional scouts might offer. New stadiums with lush green grass infields and deep red brick dust pitching mounds began filling with folks willing to pay, even during the Depression years, to enjoy the game in living color.

Brothers in Baseball

Believe it or not, the tiny railroad town of Norcross boasted sixteen players signing professional baseball contracts between 1910 and 1950—more than any other town, per capita, in the good old United States of America. Two sets of brothers, Ivey and Al "Red" Wingo and Roy and Cleo Carlyle, played in the Major Leagues, while Troyce Cofer played a season of AAA baseball for the Atlanta Crackers and Jack Trimble enjoyed several seasons with the Black Crackers.

In the late nineteenth century, Norcross players learned the game on the open lot at the bottom of a steep hill about a block from the railroad depot. Originally, this ground was the athletic field for both the middle and high schools. Students played football and baseball here, and Norcross virtually shut down on Saturdays and Wednesday nights so that everyone could enjoy a pickup or amateur league game.

It began with boys playing on a sand lot and evolved into something much bigger, thanks to the growing popularity of professional baseball. Local players with a strong arm or a big bat were signed to play professional ball.

Much of the town's success is credited to Edwin "Pop" Dean, who brought scouts to Norcross with the hope of signing talented youngsters, many of them brothers, including the Garmons, Trimbles, Davenports and Adamses.

"In those days, baseball didn't pay very much," John Adams fondly recalls of his years of playing for a semi-professional team sponsored by the National Biscuit Company, known now as "Nabisco." The company sold some of baseball's first concessions, offering cake and cracker products from a horse-drawn wagon.

Adams's wife, Martha Miller Adams, remembers that her young husband, nicknamed Big John for his tall stature, "didn't bring home much cash from

Remembering Norcross

Absalom "Red" Wingo, pictured eighth from the left in this 1916 club team photo, began a professional career with the Philadelphia Athletics in 1919. *Courtesy of the Norcross Old Timers Baseball Association.*

playing baseball, as he was paid mostly with fruitcakes and dinners from a sponsoring restaurant."

Martha admits, "A meal or a fruitcake meant quite a lot in those days."

The careers of players hailing from Norcross are retold in a collection of newspaper clippings, old photographs, autographed baseballs and personal artifacts that the Old Timers Baseball Association has collected and displayed in glass cases tucked under the steps of city hall. Between the lines of the museum's yellowed clippings, many interesting tidbits record ties to Norcross families.

One collection of clippings details an event on July 4, 1929, that lives on in record books today. On that day, Roy Carlyle hit the longest home run in professional baseball history, listed in the *Guinness Book of World Records*, while playing for a minor league team in Oakland, California. Roy walloped a fastball thrown by Ernie Nevers (a former Stanford University All-American fullback playing baseball for St. Louis) that left the park and landed on a roof outside the stadium. Witnesses noted the point of impact, a still visible dent in the gravel rooftop, and then carefully measured the distance at 618 feet.

Cleo Carlyle played for the Boston Red Sox in 1927 and several times faced Babe Ruth, by then a New York Yankee. While warming up before a game, Ruth jacked a ball into foul territory, striking Cleo's wife, who was in the stands. Ruth came over to see if she was okay and gave her an autographed baseball. A niece, Julie Carlyle Rutkowski, inherited the ball from her uncle and brought it to the Hall of Fame's rededication ceremony in 2006. When asked whether it would remain on display, she remarked, "Everyone can take a look today. This baseball is too special to our family, it comes home with me."

Nuggets of Nostalgia

Norcross contributed a notable player to the Negro Leagues in the 1930s and '40s. Jack Trimble played for the Atlanta Black Crackers before going into military service in 1941. Old-timers recall, "Jack could really go get 'em," a reference to his swiftness in the outfield. He also played for barnstorming teams and once faced Dizzy Dean in a game during the World War II years.

In its heyday years of 1961, '64, and '65, the Norcross Nuggets, an amateur team, won the Georgia state championship and represented Norcross at the National Amateur Baseball Federation tournament in Dayton, Ohio; Detroit, Michigan; and Akron, Ohio. Although the Nuggets never brought home the national title, Carl Garner remembers the city's pride as citizens decorated the team bus with a banner announcing, "This team is from the home of the Wingos and the Carlyles: Norcross!"

As with many other boys in Norcross, Ivey Wingo learned the game by competing against amateur club teams until, in 1911, he was drafted by the St. Louis Cardinals, making his hometown proud. Along with his younger brother, Absalom (nicknamed "Red" for his flaming red hair and freckled face), Ivey was drafted in 1919 to the Philadelphia Athletics. Ivey lived his dream of playing professional baseball at a time when the sport was full of more than just athletic icons; it was plagued by gamblers, cheats and crooks.

Ivey squatted behind the plate snagging sliders and spitballs as a St. Louis Cardinal until 1915, when he was traded to the Cincinnati Red Stockings. Wingo was quick—a rarity among catchers—and had a knack for stretching doubles into triples. He hit 154 triples during his career—more than Johnny Bench and Yogi Berra combined—and he stole 87 bases. Ivey was backstop in the last game pitched by the legendary Christy Matthewson when he beat Mordecia "Three Fingers" Brown and the Chicago Cubs. It was the only game Matthewson ever pitched for a team other than the New York Giants; he had become the Reds' manager, and the duel between he and Brown was set up as a publicity stunt as a final outing in both of their careers.

Ivey's strong arm and ability to call pitches helped the Reds win the 1919 World Series, although that accomplishment was marred by the Black Sox scandal, so called because some of the Chicago White Sox players, including "Shoeless" Joe Jackson, allegedly threw the game.

Wingo retired to Norcross to live out his years a few yards from the sand lot where his career began. Ivey never came to grips with the rumors that flew in the press about the infamous game. He and other old players would sit around at the store of their fellow player, Roy Carlyle, who also returned home to Norcross for retirement. Wingo defended his own statistics as well as those of his teammates, who, as he went to his grave in the city cemetery believing, won that series fair and square.

As a boy in the 1930s, Norcross resident Junior Gant hung around Carlyle's just to hear the stories. Carl Garner, president of the Old Timers Association, has heard Gant retell how Wingo's stories "lofted in the high ceilings of Carlyle's store like smoke from the pot belly stove we gathered around to listen as he spoke of playing against 'The Babe' and Ty Cobb."

"Ivey spoke of the scandal many times," Gant can remember. "From his mouth I heard him say he did not agree with the notion that the White Sox threw the game."

Of course Wingo's opinion, as a player on the winning team, never carried much weight, even though statistically the series went to eight very close games, drawing him to conclude that the entire issue had been blown out of proportion by the press.

Ivey's innocent participation in the 1919 World Series has increased the value of his memorabilia. A check he endorsed sells for more than $1,000, but the authenticity of his original baseball card has become clouded because there are several trading cards with his name scrawled over other players' cards. Why Wingo's autograph appears on some Ty Cobb cards is a baseball mystery.

Ivey's brother, Absalom "Red" Wingo, began his career with Philadelphia in 1919 and then was traded to Detroit to play with the Tigers in 1924. The following year, the Tigers had a remarkable outfield consisting of Wingo in left, Ty Cobb in center and Harry Heilmann in right. The trio batted .370, .378 and .393, respectively, and Heilmann won the American League batting title. Red passed away in Detroit, a "hometown" he had established for himself.

Dave Barrow, Amos Martin and Kenneth Meyers played football for Oglethorpe University, a private Presbyterian college about six miles south of Norcross, when their team defeated the University of Georgia in the first game ever played at Georgia's Sanford Stadium.

A not-so-famous set of brothers, a set of twins born in Norcross in 1920, Troyce and Royce Cofer were well known in town as "Big 'un and Little 'un." Both played on the high school, town and some professional ball teams.

Troyce recalled in the book *Norcross*, written in 1999 by Irene Ewing Crapo and Martha Miller Adams,

> *As kids, Royce and I loved to play baseball. There was no money for balls so we used black tape to re-tape old balls and made our bats from hickory limbs. We made our own diamond in a pasture on Sundays as week*

days were full of school and chores. We believed Daddy stayed up at night dreaming up work for us to do.

I will never forget my high school team manager, Edwin "Pop" Dean. Pop gave my teammates and I support, encouragement, and money to travel for games all around the Atlanta area. Norcross Merchants paid for our uniforms but Pop scraped up the extra cash we needed, I think a lot of it came out of his pocket. Pop loved the game and did a lot for the boys who played baseball in Norcross. I was excited when I was drafted to play semi-pro in Spartanburg, South Carolina. I couldn't believe they were going to pay me a hundred dollars to play a game I loved so much.

Bottle Caps and Broomsticks, Nulling Tops and Taw Lines

Your crowd, maybe Poo-Doo Robertson, Speedy White or Slingshot Findley, those friends and classmates with whom you regularly run with, kneel around to 'pitch a taw line." You finger the smooth glass balls piled low in the Bull Durham tobacco sack—maybe it's a Dukes mixture, they are each so smooth. The taw feels larger than the others you slip through your fingers. Press that jewel of a taw, aggie or cat's eye, between your knuckles and the tip of your thumb. Let it catch a squint of sunlight—looks real pretty, too. Some taws are striped; some are a swirl of colors.

Go no further.

Opponents must first ask of one another, "Are we playing for fun or for keeps?" Once the two determine the significance of the game, a taw line is drawn, preferably in some smooth packed dirt, avoiding even small hills or rough spots. Norcross schoolchildren know the parking lot just east of the depot to be a fine court, used often for tournament marbles. The competitors each pour three or more of their own marbles into a row within the perimeter of taw lines. Duelers pace off about eight to ten steps to start the game with a pitch of the shooter ball. Closest to the taw line has first ups.

Shots alternate in attempts to knock a marble out of the ring. Smack your opponent's taw marble rolling out of the taw lines and you score an extra shot. If you can manage to maintain a lay-up of your shooter, plan for a better shot next time. Take turns when you miss until all six marbles are out. Shoot another game for best two out of three rights or find a new player. Marbles was one of the most competitive games; it quickly taught players that a person may be bright, but still could lose his marbles.

So many games of good clean fun can be played out in the dirt. A spinning top is good for hours of fun. Store-bought models could be purchased in

Remembering Norcross

town with shopkeepers letting you "take 'er for a test spin." Wrap a string around the top, stretch it down the sides to the bottom metal end pin, wind it up, hold the button or hook that's fixed to the other end of the string and let it rip, spinning, or "walking," it across a tabletop or sidewalk.

Make that spinner hum by carving a notch around the top of it with your pocketknife. Good for playing by yourself, tops become a crowd pleaser when you challenge someone to "null" you or you take a notion to null another's top as it spins feverously.

To "null" a top meant you tried to throw your top, as it spun from the string, onto someone else's top, as it was spinning. Hitting it on top of the top was known as "nulling" player number one.

Balloon tire bicycles began floating around town in the 1940s as children started asking Santa for them at Christmas. Class pals who got one first shared with others still waiting for one of their own, or in some cases waiting for a sibling to get one so the family could share. More fun than watching others zooming past, waving their arms, laughing aloud and hollering, was to get your turn at the helm.

Children with skates were permitted to roll along the squares of white cement sidewalks connecting home to town. Halfway down Thrasher Park's sloping sidewalk, a drainage hump allowed for hops, jumps, spills and skinned knees.

Rolling youngsters increased the thrill by forming skate trains. You guessed it: two or more skaters formed a trail of skaters holding onto one another's waists, zigzagging themselves through town. A skate train sometimes grew to ten or more skaters standing or squatting as they propelled themselves behind the leader.

Need a bigger bang? Change up the game to a bicycle skate train. That's when a bike, acting as the engine, leads a snake of wheels trailing behind it. Accidents, especially when zooming over the Thrasher Park hump, lead to bruises and broken arms.

Girls, maybe Lou Johnson or Googlew Merritt, agreed to ride on someone's handlebars looking for a tingle. Some girls would yell, "I want a turn" at the boys, or, "I'm next!" Most of the boys were charged, too, pedaling their passengers faster and faster with dresses flapping and hair whipping across the boys' faces, impairing their vision but increasing their fun.

On the open lot just at the east end of the Southern Railway freight depot, hour after hour was spent playing bottle cap baseball. With no real equipment available, a couple of buddies swung behind each store in town looking for discarded R.C. Cola, Orange Crush or Nu-Grape bottle caps. Sales of pop were limited, so the caps became a precious commodity.

Nuggets of Nostalgia

Three boys of the Simpson and Nesbit families play on "Ma" Clure's front porch with a toy gun. *Courtesy of the Nesbit family.*

Harry Nesbit enjoys a metal airplane toy he was given as a gift from one of his many uncles. *Courtesy of the Nesbit family.*

Remembering Norcross

Next, get an old broomstick and saw it off to about three feet in length. You are ready to mark the sidelines as well as the lines to determine singles, doubles, triples and home runs. Flip for first "ups." Flip for pitcher. Flip for "loser buys winner a moon pie." Bottle cap baseball is not like the real baseball that young men played on the old school fields—the bottle cap version was meant for two players.

September meant a trip to the Southeastern Fair in Lakewood, Georgia. Mr. W.D. "Walt" Flowers gathered children at school or church to ride together in the back of his truck. Walt collected some cash from everyone to cover gas and drove the group to the fairgrounds, where he would unload them just inside the gate with instructions as to a time and place to meet back up for the trip home. Betty Mitcham recalls that it was a short but fun day.

The fairgrounds offered a Tilt-a-Whirl for adventuresome types and a Tunnel of Love for the romantic ones. The Tunnel of Love was a stream dug in a path to float you and your companion past several country settings, lakes, farms and country homes. Some girls and boys would hold hands or even steal a kiss along the way. At the end of your float, a cow would kick at you, ringing the bell hooked to her hoof and signaling the end of the ride. If things were going well on the first float you may run, get more tickets and take your sweetheart for another waft along the man-made waterway!

Concessions of candied apples, hot dogs, cotton candy and popcorn made for hard choices to children with limited cash. Sideshows were worth a look, perhaps a nickel, but seemed good fun, as you had the option of throwing real baseballs at milk bottles or, at the dunking booth bull's eye, sending some boy tumbling into a tank of water.

Time flew at the fairgrounds, and before you knew it the day had passed and it was time to meet up with Mr. Flowers for the trip home, sharing stories of daring adventure all the way.

In town, within walking distance for most, many forms of entertainment came and went over time. Locals walked up to the high school auditorium, where movies were shown for an admission price of ten cents until, about 1940, Bill Aiken opened the Swan Theatre. Run later by a Mr. Zebell, the Swan featured picture shows playing to crowds who also enjoyed feature nights like "dish night," a popular evening of potluck dishes, and a Bingo night. As regular weekly entertainment, the movie show was a place for the youth of Norcross to see and be seen. The last reel ran in 1950, when the Masonic lodge took over the building. As the theatre closed its doors, many original theatre seats went home with folks who needed a token of their youth. A few of the Swan's seats sit quietly in barns and sheds around town.

Nuggets of Nostalgia

Right: Summers were spent on the Chattahoochee River. *Courtesy of the Nesbit family.*

Below: Teens of the 1930s enjoyed the waters of the Chattahoochee River while on campouts. *Courtesy of the Nesbit family.*

Remembering Norcross

A bowling alley was popular for a short time in the '50s in a building still standing on the corner of Cemetery and South Peachtree Streets, used over time as a hardware store and later as an Italian restaurant.

Away from town, young people of the 1920s and '30s made their way, walking or by wagon ride, over to the Chattahoochee River, setting up camp along its banks on the farms of the Simpsons, Medlocks, Summerours, Jones or McClures. Accompanied by older uncles and aunts, teenagers swam in the icy cold river, fished for trout or spread themselves to sunbathe on many large rocks speckling the stream. Tents were pitched, campfires were stoked and folks brought meals, and sometimes servant cooks, from home, eating off china plates with silver and glassware, making this type of camping quite an event.

Martha Simpson remembers camping as a teenager with her aunt chaperoning:

> *I would ride with my aunt from our home in town but there would be a lot of people my age, both girls and boys. We had our share of fun with no one around for miles, eating berries when we could, picking apples, just swimming in our bloomers. We spent long summer days on the river. No one looked forward to returning to school after those great summers, but even away at college, my friends and I planned our breaks at camp.*

A popular path to the chilly water's bank was along Old Alabama Road, no more than a double trough, carved by wagon wheel, leading to Jones Ferry crossing. Large groups camped just east of the section of river over which Fulton and Gwinnett Counties built Jones Bridge, oak boards laid over a steel framework. When the bridge gave way in the '30s, officials never agreed on who should repair it and it sat unused until World War II, when half of the bridge was cut away for scrap, leaving bare pilings protruding on the Gwinnett side. For decades, teenagers dared one another to jump off the rusting skeleton until access from the shoreline was blocked.

STOREFRONTS

As work on the railroad lines continued, Norcross bustled with one-stop shopping. In 1890, R.O. Medlock began construction on several brick structures along both Jones and South Peachtree Streets. The brick buildings with street-level storefronts and upstairs office space housed, over time, mercantile stores, restaurants, hotels, churches, blacksmiths, livery stables, physicians, postal and fire service, the Swan Theatre and eventually even a bowling alley, all within a few steps of the depot. In those early days, farm folks rode or walked to trade goods and services while dodging the chickens, goats and cows that roamed the downtown freely.

Sylvester Cain purchased the standard railroad building at the corner of Jones Street from its first owner, Mrs. McKinney. Number 7 Jones Street had a third rail sidetrack, long since pulled up, running alongside it. Cain was shrewd in coming up with inventive early marketing efforts. One idea inspired the dropping of chickens and turkeys from the rooftops of his store. Cain enlisted the services of boys with nicknames like "Saltine" Jackson, "Frog" Davenport and "Cat Eye" Langford to toss the birds. "Doodie" Verner, "Speedy" White or "High Pockets" Johnson scrambled to snag one of the flapping fowl flying feathers downward to the street below. If they could get a firm hold on a live bird, it was theirs to keep. Spinning the bird around by its scrawny neck until dead, axing off its head, dropping the carcass into a pot of boiling water and plucking loose a thousand feathers were not included in the bargain, but it made for a fresh Sunday dinner.

Thomas Johnson's store stacked notions and potions up and down the tall shelves propped against the ten-foot walls in his store at 15 Jones Street. Originally Martin and Johnson's, the partnership dissolved amicably in 1899, when each man, equipped with a large basket, browsed the store filling his

Left: R.O. Medlock was the builder of many shops and homes in Norcross that are currently listed on the National Historical Registry. *Courtesy of Evelyn Norman.*

Below: Garner's Grocery store moved onto Buford Highway after the train no longer stopped in town, about 1950. *Courtesy of Carl and Joan Garner.*

Nuggets of Nostalgia

wicker work until each was satisfied. Johnson's store became a family tradition on Jones Street, with decades' worth of merchandise accumulating in crates or dusty corners. Johnson would sift past cobweb-covered bottles, preserved copies of *Grier's Almanac* and Civil War relics, using a long "reaching" hook, if needed, to locate a customer's requested item.

Over at Garner's Grocery, separated from Johnson's for many years by an open alley, a child lucky enough to have a nickel burnin' a hole in his pocket was quickly enticed to spend it on a colorful assortment of sweets stuffed in glass jars glistening through the front window. Favored were little round chocolate patties filled with a lush cream. Most of the rich dark cocoa candies offered a white filling, with an occasional pink filling surprising the taster's lips. Discovers of pink filling were rewarded with a small toy prize pulled from behind the proprietor's cash register.

The atmosphere along Jones and South Peachtree Streets was lively and boisterous, sometimes leading to a ruckus, making a trip to town an event. Many ladies who were school girls in the '20s, '30s and '40s grin at the memory of walking to the store for a simple pair of socks.

Anita Andrews was a child during the 1930s when her family lived in a small home in a valley of the Warbington farm along Holcomb Bridge Road. Anita calls to mind the day a traveling photographer came around offering to take pictures for folks with the newest of photographic technology. It was commonplace for knife and scissor sharpeners, chimney sweeps or sellers of medical elixirs to travel the countryside with wagons full of wares soliciting folks sitting out on their porches. Anita remembers,

> *We wanted a picture but Momma didn't have any money to pay the man. Well, Mrs. Bertha Warbington always bragged about me being a beautiful child and she offered my mother the money so they could get a picture of me. I went to pose on the porch when mother realized my socks were dirty and all my clean pairs hung dripping wet on the clothesline. Momma told the photographer that she couldn't let me get a picture wearing dirty socks! With that Mrs. Warbington sent a black woman who was working in her home up to town just to buy me a new pair!*

Hattie McClendon's family harvested crops, butchered meat and constructed their barns and homes out of stones and wood that they collected themselves, so she knew a trip into town was for special items.

"We bought coffee, sugar, pipe tobacco and pure white cotton bobby socks at the stores in Norcross," Hattie looks back. "I only wore those delicate socks with my Sunday best clothing to church or if we rode the trains into Atlanta."

Remembering Norcross

The three original storefronts along Jones Street were built in the 1880s. *Author's collection.*

A most friendly atmosphere was interrupted occasionally, a result of moonshine or the loss of control of horse or auto, sometimes leading to a serious incident.

Tucked away from the hustle of the city's streets, in an alley between Garner's Grocery store and Johnson's, Abe Johnson would set up his checkerboard and enlist a worthy opponent. Abe was consumed in one such competition when something spooked two mules carting the wagon that a teenaged Reps Miller was trying to lead away from the corn mill of Arthur Maloney. The hapless unheeding pair of young mules charged recklessly down Checkers Alley kicking game pieces, game boards, empty milk bottles, bins full of coal, scoops for the coal, chickens escaping pens, glass bottles of Orange Nehi and the chair in which Abe was sitting skyward in a dusty whirlwind.

After the mess was swept up and the young Miller boy reprimanded for his disregard of the public peace, Abe announced, "I'm tired of dodgin' wagons on my own property so I'm thinking I'll wall the alley in and that'll stop the wagons and horses and mules from passing through." He vowed

Nuggets of Nostalgia

Horse and carriage were the mode of travel on Norcross dirt streets well into the twentieth century. *Courtesy of the Nesbit family.*

to stop the unsettling hoof and foot traffic. Not long after the incident, a brick wall was laid at both ends of the busy breezeway. "Checkers Alley" sits silently encased within brick and mortar retail space.

Just east of Garner's Grocery's parking area was a small metal building that held the city's fire truck—not a fire engine, just a work truck loaded with a hose, a reel and an axe. The truck acted mostly as an efficient way to pull a water hose connected with a hitch. The front door of this building was kept locked, but if anyone discovered a fire around town they could break out the small glass pane in the door, reach inside, undo the latch, grab the keys (left hanging within reach of anyone) and flip a switch to sound the siren. The fire bell sat atop Garner's store and was so tremendously loud that it could be heard all over town, alerting every citizen into action. Later, Norcross organized a volunteer fire department and trained several residents for specific emergencies. The city built a true fire station, number one in Gwinnett County, on the Adams' blacksmith old lot on College Avenue.

William "Scrapper" Morrow made a reasonable living for himself and his wife, Sarah Terrell, as a house painter in Norcross. Morrow—along with other full-time scrappers like brothers Frank and Harry Langford, Willie Robertson, Hugh Moulder and Tom Ivy—used bristle brushes to whitewash the wood-framed homes. The paint was a thick heavy mixture of oils and lead, with premixed buckets of the chemical-laden stuff being first introduced in 1867. House painters would often build makeshift scaffolds around a structure, putting it "under the brush." Homeowners had the option of picking from a color palette, a stack of cards with primary colors that was used after the Civil War to allow for more choice in the sales of manufactured paints.

One fascinating self-employed worker around town and the surrounding countryside was Ed Brookes, a well digger and "cleaner outer." Brookes dug many of the wells used before the 1930s, when water began being piped around town by the city waterworks plant. Brookes used a windlass to clean an existing well or dig a new well. The windlass had a large wooden barrel-shaped roller supported by stanchions. Each roller had a handle, allowing people to assist him in turning the roller and therefore moving the attached rope, tied to a bucket, scooping up dirt or other obstructions from the bottom depth of the well. Ed worked alone but enlisted the help of the homeowner or hired helper. When cleaning an old well, it would be necessary to drain out any water at the bottom until the water was shallow enough for him to work. Each well, of course, was replenished by a differing source, either a spring or close flowing river or creek, so it was important for the helpers to continually wind up, often at a rapid pace, the rollers to withdraw the incoming water as Brookes worked. Water wells required cleaning every two years, as silt and soil would accumulate, clouding the water.

During dry seasons, as in the summer, Ed Brookes may have needed to dig a well deeper and deeper until hitting a flow of water. Safety came first for this well-digging professional, as he kept a rope tied around his waist securing him to an object above ground, often a tree or a barn. The rope, kept separate from the twine of the rollers, allowed helpers to pull Brookes up and out quickly in the event of a dangerous release of natural gas or cracking of his head on a protruding rock. These instances left the well digger unable to help himself, often causing him to lose consciousness. Brookes carried on his work well into the '30s, when almost every home was hooked onto the city pipes.

Shootouts

From the days of the early settlers of 1820 through the decades after the turn of the twentieth century, law enforcement around Norcross and much of Gwinnett County consisted of a deputy or a chief of police sworn in through the county seat in Lawrenceville, where superior courts were held. These early officers' duties often overlapped with chores on a farm, keeping up a shop or bootlegging behind the barn. Offenders could as easily receive justice from a judge's gavel as they could at the hands of a vigilante.

An unusual occurrence at Johnson's store, 5 Jones Street, during the 1930s happened after Police Chief Homer Green had retired to his home. As the evening engine roared and whistled through the center of town, a group of robbers backed a truck up over the curb, smashing into the storefront window. No one heard the glass shatter or saw the thieves openly load up an assortment of items undetected. In the morning, after word got around, witnesses reported seeing the truck and the men the night before but not thinking anything of it, assuming the men were making a late-night delivery. The culprits were never apprehended.

Some years earlier, a more serious circumstance transpired on Christmas Day 1915. City shops were, as was customary, open for business. This may be why so many prominent citizens bore witness to the holiest of day's fatal turn of events. A disagreement of undetermined cause stirred between Bija Nuckolls and Henry "Doc" Lively inside the apothecary of Dr. A.H. Lietch. It was not unlike Doc to stir up an argument, as he often threw punches or verbally dogged many men. The disagreement escalated as the two tousled their way down South Peachtree Street. Townsfolk watched the contentious confrontation persist until the feuding men each brandished a weapon in front of Greer-Ivy's Hardware, some distance away. In broad daylight, on

Law enforcement was minimal—perhaps one sheriff or deputy for hundreds of acres of countryside surrounding the few towns developing along the railroad lines. *Courtesy of Garland Sexton.*

a busy city street, Doc Lively, a reputed bully of great disrespect in the eyes of most, allegedly aimed his pistol at Bija, a respected butcher for Garner's Grocery. Bija managed to shoot first, and Doc collapsed to his death in an alleyway leading to the rear of the hardware store. Bija laid his shotgun down in the street, inviting numerous onlookers to arrest him. Norcross deputy Davis appeared to escort Bija to the calaboose, but Chief Allen Sudderth, holder of the only key, was not on duty, so Nuckolls remained free until sometime later, when he was taken to the county jail in Lawrenceville and confined until trial.

Authorities were unable to produce Lively's "threatening" pistol at the trial, but many eyewitnesses confirmed Bija's story, and he was found guilty of involuntary manslaughter. He appealed and was subsequently released. Many years later, a store three fronts down from the hardware store where Lively was killed underwent some remodeling. As workers stripped away the existing walls, a pistol was discovered in a crack of a wall. Bud Welch of the Norcross Police Department responded. Welch quickly put two and two together, saying, "That's Doc Lively's pistol."

It was now apparent that someone, during the confusion of the incident, had hidden the threatening weapon in the wall—or was Doc lucid enough to do it himself? Bija Nuckolls never saw this proof of self-defense.

Just five months after Doc took a fatal bullet, near the mill in an area now used as a maintenance barn by the city, the public peace was again disrupted, and this time Police Chief Allen Sudderth was involved in a shootout with Jeff Staples in the area behind the storefronts near the corn mill. The chief was seriously wounded and Staples was killed.

Along with jovial parties and family gatherings, the home of Tom Ray witnessed a tragedy. At the age of twenty-two, Thompson Blanton Ray, one of Tom's sons, was shot, for certain reasons lost in local lore, and killed. Old-timers heard the senior Ray speak often of the night he heard a knock on his front door. When he answered the knock, his son collapsed dead in the front foyer. The young man had been shot and then "returned" to his family's home. With no certainty of association, it is worthy to note that a series of money bag robberies, crushing the local economy, ceased after this deadly evening. Money and mail bags were hung on hooks along the tracks to be swooped up or dropped off by trains as they passed. On several occasions, bags were swiped down by the wrong hands, and each event was rectified by some form of vigilante justice.

For more than eighty years, a cloud of mystery has lingered around the shooting death of two prominent Norcross brothers, Joe and Orion Simpson. Their living descendants still try to put two and two together. The Simpson brothers, sons of Dr. O.O. Simpson, a well-respected physician and a representative in the state legislature serving several terms, farmed the family's property located between Norcross and Duluth in an area that would become Pleasant Hill Road. The Simpsons may or may not have been bootleggers—most old-timers say that they were—but everyone agrees that the two did not deserve to leave this life in the violent way that they did, certainly not at the hands of a "part-time deputy, part-time farmer."

Circumstances were conflicting, depending on who told the story. The truth lies somewhere in the details that piece together like this, taken from the *Gwinnett Journal*, Wednesday, February 22, 1922:

> *February 20, 1922—Joe and Orion Simpson, brothers, farmers in Gwinnett County were shot and killed by Deputy Sheriff Victor Dowis when they refused to allow the officer to search their automobile for whiskey. Dowis surrendered to higher authorities and after a search of the automobile*

> no moonshine was found. Dowis apparently received a tip, some may say a set-up, that someone was loading the booze by the barrel in to an automobile just outside the limits of Duluth, Georgia. Dowis tracked down the auto and attempted a search. The Simpsons refused on the grounds that Dowis had not sought a proper warrant and Dowis sent for such. When the warrant was presented the brothers asserted that the document was bogus and forced the officer out of their vehicle. Eye witnesses state that Dowis drew his pistol and started shooting. Orion was killed instantly and his brother Joe was shot in the back as he tried to run away. As his life slipped away from the mortal wound, Joe swore to the folks, who'd gathered in him up, "We had no whiskey."

State Senator O.A. Nix, acting as attorney for Dowis, was quoted in the *Atlanta Constitution* on February 21, saying,

> *Dowis, marshal at Duluth, was requested to search the Simpson automobile by a citizen of the county. He went to investigate the report and the Simpsons requested a warrant. Dowis returned with the required warrant to find the men had been drinking—one was half drunk—and they attacked Mr. Dowis. Eye witnesses tell me one of the Simpsons struck Dowis over the head with an automobile wrench at which point Dowis drew his pistol and shot in self-protection. I will ask for bail within the next day or so.*

After holding the deputy for a short time, the state's attorney's office found no grounds for trial, concluding that Dowis had shot in self-defense. Standing on the steps of the Lawrenceville Courthouse, Dr. O.O. Simpson was so openly angry about Dowis being found innocent that he offered up "a reward of $10,000 [a fortune in the 1920s] to anyone who would kill Vic Dowis."

A large assembly of mourners, an estimated two to three thousand, attended the Simpsons' funeral, an indication that they bore a fine reputation.

Dowis, aware of the threats on his life, moved his family to Kentucky, but not wanting to "live on the run," as he told his family, he returned six months later to his Duluth farm. Before the year was out, and just a week after his wife had a baby, Dowis went to plow a low-lying field near the Chattahoochee River. At the age of seven, Hannah "Lola" Dowis Teague, Vic's younger sister, was an "earwitness." Lola heard Vic tell their mother, "It's good weather to plow and plant pumpkins, but I doubt I will eat any pumpkin pie."

Lola, interviewed in 2000 by family members researching the events, was recorded as saying,

Nuggets of Nostalgia

I heard two gunshots go off in the field where Vic was plowing. And two of my older brothers went to check the situation. Mother told me to go upstairs to my bedroom in the back of house and remain there until she called. Instead, I went upstairs and stood on the front balcony where I saw my brother's bloody lifeless body carried inside. After that day I followed mother's instructions exactly.

Although Alexander Hamilton Simpson Sr., Joe and Orion's brother, allegedly collected the reward money, the truth did not come out until he gave a deathbed confession to his sons, Weyman, Paul and Alex Jr., who were just children when Deputy Vic Dowis was shot. Alex Sr. recanted his original testimony, admitting that he had been plowing in his fields but revealed that he had hired many hands to work his fields so he could slip away, unnoticed, to Duluth with a double-barrel shotgun over his shoulder. Before he left this world to face Peter at the pearly gates, he confessed to his sons how he hid behind a fence on Dowis's farm along the Chattahoochee River, waiting for Dowis to turn his mule and come into view and, with both barrels loaded, shot Dowis twice, in what Simpson himself described as "an attempt to blow his head off." Simpson claimed that he then returned home, only taking twenty to forty minutes to complete the task his Uncle O.O. had called for. He instructed his farm hands to offer an alibi if questioned by authorities, which they did. Although Alex cashed in on the reward money, family lore suggests that he was most likely blackmailed, as he died with little to show of it.

Joe and Orion Simpson were well known in Norcross and served in the army during World War I. One wartime comrade of Orion's, John Casey, became a music teacher, often heard singing a tune he wrote to mark the untimely passing of his friends.

"Ode to Joe and Orion Simpson"

Joe and Orion Simpson
The boys are dead and gone.
The slayer was Vic Dowis,
He was free from harm.

It was on a Monday evening,
The boys had started home.
When the car ran out of gasoline,
and the preacher came along.

Remembering Norcross

He had started with the children
to play a game of ball.
He stopped to call his brother, Vic,
And that was what caused it all.

Vic drove his car beside them,
smoking his cheap cigar.
He said, "Stand around you Simpson boys,
I am bound to search your car."

He pulled out his pistol,
And shot both boys dead.
And turned to Bill McGee,
"Are you my friend?" he said.

The judge passed the jury,
You bet he ever failed.
But how his heart will quiver,
when he meets Vic Dowis in Hell.

Hope Wells from Slavery's Shackles

Jesus said, "Whoever drinks the water I give him will never thirst. Indeed, the water I give him will become in him a well of water springing up into eternal life."

Unique among Britain's American colonies, Georgia prohibited slavery as a matter of public policy. However, as a result of the growing wealth of the slave-based plantation economy, Georgia overturned its ban. From 1750 to 1775, planters so rapidly imported slaves that the enslaved population grew from fewer than five hundred to approximately eighteen thousand. Georgia planters imported slaves chiefly from rice-growing regions of present-day Sierra Leone, the Gambia and Angola. These Africans were experienced in rice culture and brought their techniques to the colony, where they were instrumental in the success of the commodity production. Slaves worked the fields in large cotton plantations, and the economy of the state became dependent on the institution of slavery.

While there were also many smaller cotton plantations, the proportion of slaves was lower in north Georgia than in the coastal counties, but it still ranged up to 25 percent of the population. In 1860, enslaved African Americans comprised 44 percent of the population of slightly more than one million.

Most of the prominent modern-day African American families of Norcross and its surrounding settlements trace their roots to slaves held on some of the more affluent farms of the area. This being true, many family Bibles record that the slaves, though not freed until after emancipation, were treated with fairness and care while being well fed and properly sheltered. Many notes reveal servants to have become "part of the family" of their white holders, a handful proudly taking the English surnames of their masters. As slaves found a foothold of freedom, most remained in the Norcross area, considering the town to be their home.

Near the Chattahoochee River, a branch of the Nesbit family, some of the "river people," farmed fields of cotton for sale, along with a medley of corn, peas, beans and other crops to feed themselves and the family of African slaves who worked both field and domestic jobs. Members of the "Negro" Nesbit family, although considered the property of the white family from whom they acquired their surname, were well treated. Descendants do not have clear knowledge of lineage, no absolute record as to how the first relative was brought to Georgia, but neither do they have information detailing any mistreatment, whippings, vicious sales to despicable owners or even an ill perception of the days in which their great-great-grandparents lived as slaves.

Hattie Nesbit McClendon was born in 1929 on a parcel of land where her family had been enslaved sometime between 1820 and 1866 by the white Nesbit family. After the Civil War, Hattie believes her family was given land by decree of the federal government, perhaps under an enactment to grant newly freed slaves ten acres and a mule.

Elementary-aged African Americans, shown here on the steps of their school, had to take a bus to Lawrenceville, a long trek from the segregated schools of Norcross. *Courtesy of Rufus Dunnigan.*

Nuggets of Nostalgia

Hattie recollects as best she can:

> *Not one of my family members ever really said anything bad about those days. I really wish I'd asked more questions about it but, as far I know, my family was treated pretty well. They worked the fields, shared the food and lived contently in the homes built by the farm's owner. After they were freed, I believe my family took the Nesbit name and as far I know they remained on the farm near the river, working the fields and inside the house just as they always had. I know they got some of the land because Mr. Nesbit, now I don't know what his first name was, gave some land to my relatives and a tenant house out in those fields, too.*

Describing the little cemetery that sits behind large, newly built homes, Hattie remembers:

> *I know that's where I was born and that's where my parents worked the fields and that's where some of my relatives are buried. My older brother and sister walked into Norcross to go to school but I was schooled at home because it was just too far, about five miles, for me to walk to Norcross from there. Because my aunts were well educated, unusual for colored women of that time, they taught me right at home.*

"As a little girl I remember dressing up, we wore white gloves and hats and all, just so we could pick up the train in Norcross and, along with my aunt, we would ride the lines into Atlanta." Miss McClendon's eyes twinkle, the memory washing over her as she speaks:

> *She took us shopping and it was big time for us children. She only knew one way by train and I don't believe it was the most direct route, but it was the way she knew and we didn't mind the ride. I remember my whole family riding the rails up to Duluth, just the next stop going north, on Sundays to visit a church there where my uncle, Columbus "Lum" Howell attended. Uncle Lum was known and greatly respected around Norcross for being a successful blacksmith, but he was an active member of a church up there and we'd, every second or third Sunday, go to services with him.*

Lizzie May McClendon, an aunt of Hattie's husband, lived and worked on the farm of Frank and Bae Neely for fifty-three years, beginning in 1938, as a way to support her two daughters after the death of her husband. Lizzie May met many notable visitors to the farm when she worked inside the main

Remembering Norcross

Sisters born in Norcross, Annie, Betty and Florence Thompson, pose for a picture in 1940. *Courtesy of Rufus Dunnigan.*

house, as the family entertained notables who traveled to the area, including Eleanor Roosevelt. Lizzie told her own family that her life was good there and said she would like to write a book called *My Life on the Neely Farm*. Hattie and her husband lived and worked on the same farm after they were married in the 1940s.

"I had chores inside the home and my husband worked the fields," Hattie recollects. "We worked there until we had enough money to buy a house right in Norcross," near the Hopewell Baptist Church, of which she is now a member.

Just south along the river from the Neely farm was the home of R. Oliver Medlock, a businessman and Mason who built many of the original structures still lining the main streets of Norcross. On July 4, 1895, Will Tucker was born to freed slaves who still lived and worked on the farm of whites who were their previous "owners." Although Tucker attended school for a short time, he once told relatives that he "learned more by watching what was goin' on and teaching things to himself."

As a boy and a young man, Will worked for many families in Norcross and Duluth. He was a hard worker, fulfilling his day job at the Sebeco Tannery and then moonlighting as a butcher, slaughtering cattle for folks. Sometime around 1925 he bought a house and lot for fifty dollars. He sold this place for a sizable profit in order to move to the farm of Tildy Liddell, a widowed family friend who was ill and needed help with the place. After Tildy died, she left the farm to Tucker, who turned his butchering skills into a barbecue business, which became the famous Rib Shack. Tucker sold soft drinks and sandwiches, and later built a fishing lake and sold licenses. If asked how he learned to cook that well, Tucker would say, "Nobody taught me, I just learned myself."

When a large thoroughfare was built right through his property, he sold out and moved back to Norcross. Tucker went on to be the first black bus driver for Gwinnett County public schools. This came about because he would load up children in the back of his truck and deliver them to school each morning and evening. The county finally gave him an old bus that he drove until it gave out. He liked fixing things and repaired the bus many times. At the time of his death in 1975, Will Tucker had forty grandchildren and twenty-four great-grandchildren.

Martha Nesbit stirs up a fond memory from her childhood of a "colored" woman, as Martha describes her, who took up living in the back pasture of her parents' home. Ollie and Anne McLure Nesbit let the woman—Martha can't recall her name—live in a small home, nothing more than a shack, in the far end of their some five acres at 297 North Peachtree Street. The four-wooden-walled and tin roof structure had a stone fire pit with a modest chimney and an area to plant a garden. Martha can picture the lady wearing a pressed white linen apron with big ruffles running down the edges whenever she came up through the yard to help Martha's mother prepare large meals. Martha doesn't think the lady worked full time for her family, as she did the laundry of many families in town and also helped with the cooking at large gatherings.

"Daddy treated her like family. She was free to come and go and do as she pleased," Martha recounts a usual occurrence at one of these large meals for many friends and family gathered in her parents' home:

> *We'd all be sitting down to eat and as folks pulled up a chair she set out bowls of food then headed to the kitchen to make her a plate saying, "I can't be sitting to eat with you good folks," but Daddy wouldn't hear of it and he would set her right down at the big table with us saying, "Oh yes you are, if I sit and eat, so do you." She sat down like Daddy told her to and ate a nice meal with any visitor, and Daddy entertained a lot of politicians, judges and even a few vaudevillians.*

Remembering Norcross

A great source of fundamental Christian fellowship for the descendants of slaves in Norcross is the two churches, Central and Hopewell Baptist, both within a community referred to as the "crack." The "crack" was actually a residence turned barroom and casino of sorts. A young John Adams rode his bike through the community in the 1920s to deliver the newspaper and was well known by the proprietors, Joe Zuber and John Henry Rodgers. Adams isn't sure if the establishment had all the proper licensing, but he knew it operated without opposition from Norcross law enforcement. A gambling game of choice was punch cards: like the in-town gambling played at Lawson's restaurant, customers "punched" a small plunger into a roll of paper, hoping to reveal a coin denomination of higher value than they had paid to play, often finding a 0 value instead of any payoff. Over time, complaints were made to the city government about the blatant gambling here and in some stores and restaurants along the main drag in town, but with so many of the elected councilmen—as well as a succession of mayors—frequent bettors themselves, the council choose to overlook complaints and took no action to shut things down for many years.

Adams recounted,

> *My deliveries carried me right through the "crack" on Frank Kelley Street every afternoon. I never had any trouble with anyone bothering me, even with them shootin' dice, punching cards or drinking liquor, right out in the open. Zuber and Rodgers often invited me in for a soda or some cookies. Cordial relationships existed between the blacks and whites in Norcross, and by the 1920s and '30s some blacks lived side by side with whites in houses on Academy and Cemetery Streets behind the business district, and I knew of a few whites who lived in, what I guess you'd call the Hopewell area, in houses next door to blacks. It was this way on the street where I lived, across the tracks and behind my dad's blacksmith shop, it was considered to be a white community but two of our most cherished neighbors were from a black family living right next door. An attitude of harmony existed, and as far as I can remember, Norcross never has had any problems with violent racial behavior directed toward anyone.*

Hopewell Baptist Church was the moral opposite of the illegal activities of the "crack." Parishioners sought to uplift the reputation of the community and attempted to clean up much of the area. Organized by slaves freed shortly after the Civil War about 1865, Hopewell was forced to reorganize after a fire in 1920 left the early meetinghouse and all of its records in ash. The congregation held services in a white framed building on Hunter Street until 1947, when it began work on a building to be constructed with granite from Stone Mountain, a solid monolith east of Norcross, drenched in Native American folklore and Civil War history, including its famed carving of Jefferson Davis, Stonewall Jackson and Robert E. Lee on horseback. The rock's summit reaches eight hundred feet above the surrounding landscape, from which you can see for miles. The granite mass spans more than nine miles in every direction from its center and is an example of "solid ground." Early deacons of Hopewell—Estes Dunnigan, Will Tucker, Clifford Bailey, Jordan Craft and Andrew Smith, among others—oversaw this undertaking until its completion nearly five years later.

Membership at Hopewell grew exponentially after Pastor William Shields accepted the call to lead the flock. In 1983, the congregation had collected nearly $170,000 toward the renovation of the stone church. During this expansion, Hopewell developed a close alliance with the Christ Church Episcopal congregation housed in the old First Baptist building across from Thrasher Park. That cooperative use of the sanctuary was reciprocated by the Hopewell members with donations of money to the Episcopal congregation for the use of utilities and space. At a combined meal celebrating the completion of Hopewell's larger building, the Episcopal membership returned the monies given as a gesture of community fellowship.

The church congregation quickly outgrew its building, and by 1993 the construction of the City of Hope—a five-acre complex complete with an athletic facility, a Christian academy and a new sanctuary—was well underway. Visitors enter the complex under large arches welcoming them to "God's Glory." The City of Hope cleaned up a part junkyard that had taken over a sizeable lot at the corner of Autry and West Peachtree Streets.

Central Baptist is the fruit of the labor of Mrs. LeRoy N. Nesbit and Reverend W.L. Jones. Working together, the two organized a service on October 4, 1904, with Reverend A.W. Williams pasturing his first flock in a blacksmith's shop near Medlock Bridge Crossing. On June 4, 1905, the congregation of twelve members purchased property and a building on the top of Autry Street but only held a few meetings at that location, as they quickly discovered that the deed for the land was improper and invalid. Dr. Walker purchased the land around the church and found inconsistencies in his plat. Dr. Walker graciously gave the membership fifty dollars and the building, which was rolled downhill from the first lot to its present location closer on Autry Street to West Peachtree Street on a lot given by Mrs. Izze Williams.

It was the first day of the year 1943 when the building burned. With no insurance and nothing saved, the minister resigned. Central members, some having been at the church for generations, carried on as a congregation and through the help of the community met in a new building on the second Sunday of October the same year. Martin Luther King Sr., pastor of an Atlanta church, preached at the dedication sermon. Of the membership were many graduates of Morehouse, Spellman and Tuskegee Colleges. Mrs. Izze Williams and Mrs. Ruby Nesbit Weaver held places on the board of the National Convention of Baptist Churches.

Over the years, both churches have struggled, but since the 1980s, Hopewell has flourished in the community with a large active fellowship maintaining numerous outreach programs. Central sold its land and building facility to assimilate the Hopewell campus, moving the congregation to a new location in Lilburn, Georgia.

Even during the active days of the local chapter of the Ku Klux Klan, neither whites nor blacks took that club to be a "hate" group, as its well-earned reputation denotes today, although Rufus Dunnigan, representing the fifth generation of slave descendants, says he "didn't go down to the park on that day [when the KKK members were gathered]. I was nervous." Rufus's mother, Annie Trimble, was the sister of Jack Trimble, of black baseball fame. Rufus's father, Estes, was employed in Norcross for many years at the Sobeco Tannery and later employed by the United States Envelope Company in Doraville, Georgia, an area closer to the Mechanicsville settlement. Estes was a deacon at Hopewell for over sixty years.

Active between 1920 and 1940, Colonel John Adams recalls that the Klan was "not [a group] everybody talked about, but everybody knew about." The Klan of Norcross was known mostly as a group that helped those who needed a hand, not a havoc-wreaking hate group viciously lynching blacks. The Klan had two leaders who served terms as mayor of Norcross, with many other Norcross locals working at the robe factory at the state headquarters, at that time located in Buckhead, Georgia, in a brick structure now known as the Exchange Building. It was no secret who were members, as the club's band marched around Thrasher Park, in uniform, to a crowd that consisted, coincidentally, of both cheering whites and blacks. No rumor or proof of any harmful action attributed to the Klan has ever slipped from the lips of either a black or white person who calls Norcross their home.

Before the 1950s, black teens had no local high school that they were allowed to attend. The nearest school at that level for Norcross blacks was in Duluth, and many folks remember an old bus they had to ride up there in.

Nuggets of Nostalgia

High school students are shown in a class photo sometime before desegregation in the 1950s. *Courtesy of Rufus Dunnigan.*

Remembering Norcross

Rufus Dunnigan recalls,

> *That old bus broke down on the side of road, if it started at all, more days than it ran. Some days it took all morning just to get to school. I remember we felt so sorry for that driver and so lucky to make it at all.*
>
> *When a desegregated Norcross Elementary opened in the 1950s, a lot more African American children were able to attend school.*

State patrolmen were on hand to escort the blacks into the school. Many of those first students, including Anne Barker (an African American student) and Jimmy Nesbit (a white student), remember the buildup to that day.

"Cops were lined up all over the downtown roads," Nesbit reports. "But none of the problems, like we had heard of in other states, happened."

"Nobody caused any trouble, and we just went into school and got started," Barker notes. "I was already friends with a little white girl that walked most of the way to school with me when we had to split up to go into our own school buildings. I was excited to enter Norcross Elementary because we could walk in together and leave together for home in the afternoon."

From Books to Bandages to Bazaars

Ladies of Norcross, specifically members of the Woman's Club, first envisioned a permanent library building for their growing town in 1907, when there was a statewide call for all clubs to observe Library Day by donating at least one book to their local library. The Norcross group manifested an unusual enthusiasm for the project, appealing to Edward Buchanan, a successful businessman and Norcross native living in New York, who donated a starter seed amount of $100 in July of that year. Norcross businessmen multiplied the incoming contributions and the ladies purchased a set of New International Encyclopedias. Many citizens donated from their own collections of books and the library made "a brave beginning," with shelves stacking three hundred books ready for checkout in a small room of the public grade school. On the first afternoon of operations, records reveal that seventeen books were checked out by the hands of its first librarian, Miss Harriett Webster, a woman with an appropriate last name for a librarian.

In September 1907, Mr. and Mrs. Homer Jones traveled to New York to thank Buchanan for his donation and explained how far his money had gone. Future plans were detailed to the entrepreneur, who was so impressed that he called for his checkbook and wrote out an amount of $2,500 for the purpose of furthering plans for a permanent library building, or, as Buchanan is remembered saying, "so Norcross can have a library building of its own." The check was deposited in a secure fund until a lot could be purchased and building plans resolved.

In 1909, the library moved to a rent-free room at the Masonic lodge along South Peachtree Street, at which point the Woman's Club, under the direction of librarian Miss Sophia Myers, decided to make the facility a subscription library, requiring folks to pay ten cents a month in order to

Remembering Norcross

Many ladies of the Norcross Woman's Club collected funds to build and stock the shelves of the town's first library. *Courtesy of the Nesbit family.*

check out books as members. This plan was not successful, and in February 1910 it regained public access.

In August 1910, Buchanan, once a millionaire, fell upon great misfortune and found himself penniless. In a letter to the Woman's Club, he implored their understanding and begged that they lend the funds he had donated previously to an account to help his foster mother retain her large home, known as the stone house, across the corner from Thrasher Park. The club consented and, not wanting to embarrass the Buchanan family, transferred money for the home until a deed could be executed and the club could recoup the funds at an interest rate of 8 percent. In 1915, litigation was completed and the club recovered its funds, plus interest, as agreed, now totaling $4,131.97. Members thought it wise to hold off on plans to build a separate library building, thinking it would overstretch available funds as costs for labor and material were not concrete.

However, after a vote of the membership, a lot sitting along North Peachtree Street across from Thrasher Park was purchased from John Simpson. The future library site was dedicated with a prayer for God's

Nuggets of Nostalgia

The first library building is now used as a country store and meeting place for the Woman's Club. *Author's collection.*

blessings, but ground was not broken until April 1, 1920. The laying of a cornerstone on June 18, 1921, culminated the great resolve of the club, whose efforts were rewarded when the Norcross Library opened in September 1920. Refreshments were served.

The contents of the cornerstone included a list of city officials who held office at the time, a list of all church pastors, a list of bank officials, the name of postmaster W.M. McElroy, a written history of the Woman's Club, its creed, the library efforts to that point in time, a Confederate bill, a United States flag, a Confederate flag, a silver coin and a Bible. Everyone who participated in great and small ways felt pride in the building's fulfillment of the hopes and dreams of the early visionaries, especially after so many years of disappointments and setbacks. Library doors opened up to some 2,500 shelved books.

The Woman's Club continued to meet in the library building, recording several interesting minutes, including the introduction of a new product, Clorox bleach, which Mrs. Ben Summerour recommended the book committee sell as a fundraiser contributing to the paving of Cemetery Street. One notation records the reading of a proclamation by then Governor of Georgia Clifford Walker to name March as "Cow-Hog-Hen Week." Over

Curtis Nesbit, son of Noye Nesbit, returns from World War II. He married Martha Simpson and the two prominent families were forever joined. *Courtesy of the Nesbit family.*

the years, the ladies donated trees in memory of deceased soldiers; gave a Victrola to the tuberculosis hospital in Milledgeville, Georgia; and purchased a complete set of Fuller brushes for the recorded purpose of dusting the library's books.

Changing social climates sometimes stirred paranoid scrutiny of club members, apparent when Mrs. A.A. Kelly spoke on the subject "Can you prove you're an American," urging the women to ready their birth certificates in preparation for an emergency. Another discussion in 1910, while the group was still meeting at the Masonic lodge, on children's hygiene, was distracted when the door of the Mason's hall was opened and ladies rushed to get a glimpse of the "Sanctum Sanctorium." Agitated by the stampede's excitement, some ladies strayed from the subject, turning the discussion to a question of propriety concerning whether a spinster should lead the Mother's Congress, a women's organization initially begun to ensure the welfare of children, but was scoffed at in the early 1900s for having members who were "old maids" and "childless."

World War II brought the temporary close of the library, and local ladies set forth an effort to join with the Red Cross, using the building as a gathering place for the rolling of bandages and the collection of items needed to aid the troops. This tenuous time in our country's history brought discussion of everything from the collecting of cooking fat, which the ladies were instructed to turn in at Kent's store, to the importance of rationing of gasoline, coffee and canned goods. Those ladies who could began knitting warm hats for distribution by the Red Cross, and it was during this era that the Woman's Club donated boxes of books and eleven lawn chairs to the Veterans Hospital in Chamblee, Georgia, just a short trip from Norcross.

In the 1950s, film projectors, artwork, phonograph records and a summer reading program encouraged children to use the library under the progressive programs of librarian Mrs. B.J. Wingo, and the library flourished once more.

The library outgrew that first early building that Woman's Club members worked so many years to complete and moved to a larger location on Carlyle Street until 1986, when voters approved the $19 million construction of a modern facility to become part of the Lanier Regional System.

The original building has been used for many civic groups over the years, with Woman's Club members setting up a country store for the browsing of holiday cookbooks and bazaar items. And yes, books of local lore are still shelved there.

Pioneer Paean

The kitchen safe stands fast by the wall, And these are the tales it could tell;
"I've seen the wood stove replaced by the range, The bucket give way to a pump in the wall.
I've heard the splash of milk in the churn, As the dasher went down with a plop.
I've smelled the milk as sweet as cow's breath, As the butter came slowly to the top.
My shelves held food for hungry mouths, Of children for many long years.
I've heard their laughter and shared their joys. I've heard their hurts and tears.
But now my days of glory are past, And give way to progress I must.
I've joined the brigade of antique things, Because my hinges are creaking with rust."
—*"The Kitchen Safe," by Alice Youngblood*

After eight decades of life experience, Miss Alice Youngblood, a self-taught writer inspired to "feel the words" by poet laureate Frank Stanton, began a recount of memories in poetry. Without much of a formal education, Alice first learned to read the Bible, *Greer's Almanac* and the Sears Roebuck catalogue, the only printed words available to her as a child. She was born in 1897 within the farmhouse that expanded by additions from the original single room built by her father, Robert Youngblood, in 1872, a year before he married her mother, Mary Haynie.

"The old house has seen a lot of love and happiness and also a lot of sorrow and sadness," Youngblood recalled in a 1987 newspaper article written in celebration of her ninetieth birthday. Youngblood was still active and sharp minded, especially as she recalled the early years of Norcross. "I prefer to remember the happy times," she noted. "I try to put the hardships on the back burner of my mind." Hardships for these early settlers included the passing of her mother when Alice was but a child of twelve years. She was the last of thirteen children born to her parents, seven of whom survived to be adults.

Remembering Norcross

Nona Simpson feeds chickens in the yard of her family's in town home. *Courtesy of the Nesbit family.*

Founding families of Norcross gathered in community fellowship at one of several Christian churches scattered about the rolling countryside. The Youngbloods were early members of Mount Carmel Methodist Church, a few miles north of Norcross toward the Pinckneyville settlement. Early parishioners walked for service one Sunday a month to hear the preacher on the Lawrenceville circuit. A faithful foundation spanning several generations of Youngbloods was depicted through personal moments of worship in her poem entitled "I Remember":

> *The old time meetin' in the old time days,*
> *The old time preacher with the old time ways.*
> *A banging out the truth to his sleepin' flock.*
> *And preachin' the hands right around the clock;*
> *"Wake up you sinners, before it's too late,*
> *Or you'll be sorry at the Judgement gate."*
>
> *No high-faludin' song, no pipe organ there,*
> *"Amazin' Grace" a-rollin' in the air.*
> *With "Rock of Ages" then the "Angel Band,"*
> *"Old Time Religion" and the "Promised Land,"*

Nuggets of Nostalgia

The wandrin sinners who were prome to oam,
Just singin' right out, "Lord I'm coming Home!"

Youngblood wrote when the mood struck her, often going days without jotting down a verse. She tended to write about the pleasant memories recorded in a booklet compiled by her great-niece for a college project entitled "Memories from the Trunk of Alice Youngblood." The title is born of the poem Alice penned.

Alone with my thoughts on a rainy night,
While the memories come stealing in silent flight.
They pass through the flicker of lamplight glow,
And leave in the silence on soft tiptoe.
To flee in the darkness of night and rain,
Like faint dying chords of an old refrain.

Many of Alice's poems detail stories she heard as a child of pioneer farm life and the period her parents' spoke of as the "War Between the States."

One story that stands out is an occasion her father experienced during the Civil War. He and his siblings were playing out in the yard of their homestead when a group of Northern Union soldiers approached on horseback and mules. The children ran into the house exclaiming to their mother, "The Yankees are coming!"

Union soldiers had a well-founded reputation for ravaging homes and taking food or livestock from innocent families who had little or nothing to do with the war. The only food Alice's grandmother had in the house was a sack of cornmeal, and thinking that this would not satisfy their pillaging, she scooped up the youngest child, filled a basin with water and, after tucking the meager portion of meal between the linens, placed the child in bed and began stroking his head with a wet cloth. A Union soldier entered the house but, unable to find anything on hand, left, saying to Alice's grandmother, "I'm sorry your little boy is sick, I hope he will be better soon." The soldiers moved on and the children, including the "sick" one, went on about their play.

Another warm recollection was an occasion when a soldier offered Grandmother Youngblood a dollar bill to purchase something. It was the first greenback she had ever seen and her reaction startled the Northern soldier. "I can't use that," she told him, "it's not our kind of money."

"Lady," the Yank responded, "you'd better take it; it's the only kind you're gonna see from now on."

Remembering Norcross

Upon accepting the dollar, she gained the distinction of being the very first person with federal money of anyone around.

The ravages of war devour the losing side, and after four years of bloodshed, dividing brother against brother, the South was despoiled and ransacked. In the end, General Sherman irreverently trampled across Georgia as he marched his troops to the sea. Of the Southerners left behind at home, most were destitute mothers of starving children forced to load their families into wagons and carts in a frantic flee to seek shelter and safety with relatives in Tennessee or South Carolina. Alice's maternal grandmother was one such refugee who traveled to Anderson, South Carolina. Youngblood's paternal grandmother, without oxen or cart, could not escape the burning line of Union cavalry, though she survived the general's trampling desecration.

Throughout her writings, Alice marvels at the fortitude and abilities of her ancestors. One such marvel was her father's single-handed process for roofing the family's barn and farmhouse. First he felled a large oak tree, removed the bark and sawed it by hand to the correct lengths; then he stood them end to end. With an axe and a tool called a mall, he split each length into quarters to be used as shingles. Youngblood rigged the slats between the logs running as main support beams. The shingles were fitted together tightly by using a long, heavy blade knife known as a "drawing knife." The drawing knife caused the planks to become tilted and wedged securely. Over time and weather, the flat boards would curl up, causing leaks, which were repaired by the mashing of mud and grass between the cracks.

Not all of Alice's memories were of work. The Youngbloods were set apart in Norcross for the social affairs hosted at their homestead. Women shared hours of conversation at quilting parties while men folk participated in corn shuckings. The ladies stirred and stewed large pots of vittles, satisfying the ravenous appetites the men built up by partaking of strong, corn-feed refreshment.

A Simple Story

The heavens are telling of the glory of God; and their expanse is declaring the work of his hands!
—Psalms 19:1

At the age of eighty-four, with a great desire for God's natural beauty to be enjoyed for generations, Miss Anna Louise "Ludie" Simpson sought to deed her family's river farm property, part of the area called Pinckneyville, to a church for the purpose of retreat—with a stipulation that the land be preserved.

The Presbyterians were first offered the prime real estate but could not agree to keep the land intact. Two years later, Miss Ludie met around her kitchen table with John O. Bishop, Jamie Mackay and Dr. Chandler Budd, all representatives of the Methodist Church. After hiking the area many times with her, everyone agreed to her wishes, and the Methodists received her generous gift, an as-yet-unnamed retreat center where visitors could find respite surrounded by God's glory, just as Miss Ludie envisioned.

Miss Ludie began a thirty-five-year teaching career with the Atlanta and Gwinnett public school systems in 1910. A world traveler, she enjoyed an active retirement, hiking, traveling, writing and enjoying her family until her death in 1975. Known to be altruistic, Miss Ludie also deeded three hundred shares of stock in the Southern Company to Mount Carmel Methodist Church and Norcross Presbyterian Church.

Gwinnett County public schools built Simpson Elementary School on property located on an adjoining section of the family's farm. The school's main office honors Ludie's generous gift in a display of personal papers, including her teaching certificate.

Grady Simpson lived in this home along what is now Thrasher Street. *Courtesy of the Nesbit family.*

Ludie was buried at Mount Carmel Methodist Church alongside her mother, Elizabeth Jane Sanders Simpson. Shortly after Ludie's funeral, John Wesley Pittman, a caretaker of the family farm, thought up the name Simpson-woods. Reflective of Ludie's simple lifestyle and love of trees, birds and small woodland creatures, Pittman and many people who knew Ludie thought she would have liked it, too. On September 25, 1985, the Simpsonwood Retreat and Conference Center was consecrated.

A stained-glass window in the Simpsonwood chapel is dedicated to Ludie's grandparents, Thomas McGregor and Mariah Jackson Sanders, who homesteaded close to an Indian trading post where the relic of a stone chimney remains on retreat property.

Pasture Golf

Golf is and has been the better part of the activities enjoyed by members of the Atlanta Athletic Club, organized in 1898 and relocated to East Lake in 1915. Amateur golfer Bobby Jones grew up playing golf at the East Lake Club. In 1960, the club moved to the pastures adjacent to the Chattahoochee River farmed by the Summerour family, designing two championship golf courses, a pool, a clubhouse and an internationally renowned tennis facility.

Interesting to note is that the athletic club was not home to the first golf stroked on the Summerour property. Late in the 1920s, the family gave permission for locals to carve out nine fairways and nine sandy mounds of greens amidst grazing cattle, sheep, horses and mules, and no doubt their droppings.

Homer Summerour acquired several hundreds of acres as his portion of an inheritance of family-owned land. He dredged the river for gold with a dredge boat he built himself, rigged a wood furnace as a steam evaporator for the conversion of sorghum cane into syrup and, in about 1904, began a conscientious and scientific project of cross-pollinating pure Cook cotton seed he ordered directly from the breeder. The new variety was advertised as "Summerour's High Linting," reaching a yield of 50 percent, hence becoming known as "half and half."

A ginner once asked him, "When I tell people what this cotton is supposed to do and they come down here and it doesn't live up to your claims, what will you do then, Mr. Summerour?"

Homer assured, "We will tear up every damn one of those lint flues and find where it went."

Homer's "half and half" holds an unbroken record as the single greatest improvement in the history of cotton. If statistics had been kept of the number of farmers who dealt at one time or another in "half and half," the figure would be in the millions.

The six hundred acres cut from Homer's farm and sold to the Atlanta Athletic Club by his son Ben in 1960 first hosted Summerour pasture golf some four or five decades earlier. Play progressed from a sandy spot, "tee-box," stroked along plowed fields, destined to plop on a sand green, eventually trickling into a tin cup. Out of bounds resulted from a ball sailing into neighboring pastures or beyond shrub fencing that divided farmland that doubled as an excellent area for quail, squirrel and rabbit hunting. A sizeable pond, dammed up at the end of an ever-flowing stream, was used as a hazard for golfers as well as a source for drinking water, a fishing pond for bream and catfish and, on Sundays, a baptismal for newly immersed local church members.

As tees were not available, pinching a tuft of grass between your thumb and forefinger, forming a mound, lifted your ball for a tee shot. Later, a new idea came about and golfers used buckets of water and sand, placed strategically about the fields, to dip and pinch sandy mounds for ball placement. Greens were also sand, and grazing animals would aimlessly depress deep footprints across them. In an effort to correct this problem, players would drag a wooden paddle, about eighteen inches wide, from the cup to their ball, allowing them to putt along the smoothed-out sandy trench path. Eventually, barbed wire was attached to short posts encircling the greens to discourage the animals' trampling.

Pasture golf required both imagination and invention. The cup was an empty can, with holes punched at the bottom to allow for drainage, sitting down several inches in the center of a green that averaged twelve to fifteen feet in circumference. Various diameters of brims on the soup to salmon cup cans, still wrapped with a fading paper label, presented a challenge for putters who preferred the Maxwell House coffee cans, boasting a distinctively wider brim, proving good to the last ball drop!

Home Shine

In 1879, plans were forming to serve liquor in a town bar, but the Baptists opposed its sale and Norcross remained officially "dry" well into the 1990s.

Sale of Coca-Cola in the restaurants and general stores was banned on Sundays, as it was thought of as an adult beverage due to the debatable trace amount of cocaine that it contained until 1902. Some folks got around this town code by paying for the fountain drink during the week and washing it down on Sunday afternoons.

Higher social circles of Norcross elite sipped moonshine on their verandas. Mommas administered a "medicinal" few drops over a teaspoon of sorghum syrup. Poor corn farmers brewed it as a moneymaker. Police Chief Homer Green managed to overlook it, at least that of a homegrown variety.

Four notorious bootleggers manufactured and sold their corn-feed moonshine within the Norcross vicinity—two operated downtown under the noses and with full knowledge of most everyone in the area, including local authorities. The four generally well-respected, God-fearing farmers carried on their activities beyond complaint of citizens, customer or not.

One activity of two such local bootleggers was not ignored. In the fall of the year, during the first run of their corn crops, the bootlegging farmers hosted a great party in their cornfields, usually near the site of the still, attended by neighbors, including folks with official titles. The first run of liquid lightning washed down a mess of Brunswick stew, hot dogs roasted at the ends of sticks, and pork barbecue pulled from a whole pig cooked over night in a deep pit in the ground. It was a great social event that many ladies attended.

Remembering Norcross

A young man of Norcross enjoys a sip while sitting on the bumper next to an Endless Caverns of Virginia wood sign on his truck. *Courtesy of the Nesbit family.*

A single documented complaint about the illicit production of moonshine was made to the grand jury of Gwinnett County. Court records show that no indictment was ever brought down. Deeper investigation discloses that a large number of jurors were from Norcross.

Mountain moonshiners passing through Norcross on their way to Atlanta did not receive the same courtesies. Chief Green occasionally caught the travelers making their way to sell the brew in Atlanta and confiscated the foreign libations. Most of the stuff was stored in rectangular metal cans that were easily stacked on the backs of their wagons. Green relieved them of their cargo, storing it in the city's calaboose. He had a good plan for getting rid of the excess whiskey. His procedure was always the same. Green, who never talked much about anything, would walk past the boys hanging around the storefronts, usually whittling or playing checkers, and say, "The moonshine is stacked to the ceiling and I have to pour some out in a couple of hours. I'll be needin' a little help from you boys."

Nuggets of Nostalgia

This signal sent everyone into action. Boys would scatter in all directions. Someone would appear at the top of the terra cotta sewer drain that ran behind the storefronts, past city hall and drained out toward the only septic area in town. The far end of the pipe was about three feet off the ground, and when it rained, water rushed over it in a waterfall. The boys knew to rinse the pipe with several buckets of well water drawn in anticipation of the chief's impending whiskey disposal.

Another group of boys gathered downhill of the drain with an assortment of empty fruit jars, pop bottles and buckets prepared to collect the anticipated alcoholic cascade. Several folks would show up at the calaboose to help carry the shine, and Green accompanied them to personally begin the pouring out part of the process. As the project progressed, folks at the lower end, just beyond eyesight of the chief, were catching the runoff as it rushed through the clean drain. Enough of the hooch was gathered that every known drinker in town could have a party for a week. This scientific disposal was obvious but ignored.

One still operated at the Adams family blacksmith shop. In 1930, Adams opened a second shop in the city of Chamblee, several miles south of Norcross, where he would travel to work three days a week. On the three working days he was away, his sons and a number of neighbors dreamed up the idea of building a portable still that operated in his absence. The black smoke that poured out of the smither's chimney was not suspicious to the average citizen, since smoke from a blacksmith's shop was considered a matter of course. The product of this community still would be divided amongst the eager volunteers. Some of the overflow was prudently stored by the bottle in the smokehouse adjacent to the blacksmith for use as a snakebite remedy.

One prominent bootlegger was a man whose wife was, at the time, in charge of the Women's Christian Temperance Union of Gwinnett County. While the wife actively made speeches and circulated literature on the evils of hooch, her husband was actively making and circulating the devil's drink of which she spoke just across the street from their home.

Another common drink of fermentation was a home brew that shared the taste and effect of beer. Produced in many kitchens, the mixture was creatively stored in bottles hidden from visitors who did not partake in the beverage. The concealed stash would sometimes become too warm, causing an explosive fermentation that revealed the family's home brew. Told and retold by Reverend A.J. Johnson, the preacher from Norcross First Baptist Church, was an occasion of a visit he made to a husband and wife who were his parishioners. The three were chatting in the living room when they

Remembering Norcross

Grady Simpson's family gathered at his house on Thrasher Street on December 25, Christmas Day 1888. *Courtesy of Evelyn Norman.*

were interrupted by a popping noise coming from the kitchen. The couple quickly recognized the sound of bottles exploding under the kitchen sink. The wife ran to survey the situation and returned to the preacher and her husband, thinking that she had resolved the problem. Just a few minutes later, however, the noise began again and the wife again ran to remedy the problem, hoping to maintain the couple's secret. The wife returned once more but the interruptive popping continued.

At this point the preacher took charge of the situation, saying, "Maybe we ought to just drink some of that home brew before it all blows up!"

Other poor farmers produced some beverages of alcoholic content by mashing the fruit of persimmon trees indigenous to Norcross. Each fall, if a harvest was plentiful, the fruit was chopped and then put to churn with water, yeast and a small amount of sugar. This type of brewed beer had a delicious taste, reflective of the portion of sugar added, and was popular for its alcohol content, which was lighter than the stilled-for-profit moonshine.

Nuggets of Nostalgia

Ma Clure enjoys her grandchildren on the porch of her home along North Peachtree Street. *Courtesy of the Nesbit family.*

Remembering Norcross

Muscadine and scuperdine grapes, plums and black- or pokeberries grown on family farms were popular mash for homemade wines. Most folks used the stuff for coughs or colds, not competing for the bootleggers' profit. "Big" John Adams recalls that his grandmother, who lived with his family during her declining years, kept a gallon jug of pokeberry wine under her bed. The elderly woman began each day with a tablespoon slurp of the fermented juice. She touted it as "a combatant of croupy cough and a tasty defense of other rheumatoid ailments."

Grandmother Adams died at the age of ninety, triggering her son to joke, "If she would have drank a full cup every day, she would have lived to one hundred!"

Apothecaries and Cemeteries

Many fine doctors, educated at distinguished universities, healed the sick and injured of Norcross.

Dr. Oliver Oglethorpe Simpson, born in 1860 on the Simpsons' river farm, attended school in Atlanta and first saw patients in a town office, and later in the front room of the home he built at 297 North Peachtree Street in 1895. He and his wife, Martha "Mattie" Rakestraw, expanded their family and built a larger home next door in 1910. Dr. Simpson was one of the first notables in town to drive an automobile, and his inability to maneuver it properly was also well known. Simpson kept an auto in the shed behind the home at 297, and when he pulled it out to drive it along the dirt roads of the town, folks grabbed up their children and moved out of his way. The doctor frequently mixed up the gears on the car, slamming into fences, trees and sometimes livestock that routinely roamed freely in Norcross. Simpson traveled to many patients by horse and buggy but his family discouraged his operation of the new-fangled automobile. He mostly kept the vehicle parked in the barn, which he sometimes referred to as the "nicest garage in Norcross." The couple's oldest son, Ollie, moved into the home at 297 when he married Anne McLure. Ollie was popular around town, playing town team baseball, and is remembered to have said, "Nothing but death could get him to leave Norcross."

Dr. W.W. Puett kept an office above the bustle of the activities in the Kent building at 7 Jones Street, a standard railroad building that, along with a mercantile, served as a warehouse for the unloading and loading of goods and livestock off the side rail that ran alongside it. He eventually moved his office to his home, the old Ray family farm, which he purchased from Tom Ray's daughter, Annie.

Remembering Norcross

Dr. Sylvester Cain grew up in the building at 7 Jones Street, as his mother operated Cain Dry Goods there. Sylvester attended Emory Medical College, graduating in 1925, and practiced medicine for the good people of Norcross from 1936 until his death in 1965. He was a much-loved part of the community, and citizens found a great opportunity to show him appreciation, in April 1955, while he was recovering from a ruptured stomach ulcer. While he was out for eight weeks, folks completely redid his office. Even schoolchildren donated their pennies to help spruce up the examination room in which Cain cared for their maladies.

Dr. Archibald Lietch was a pharmacist in Norcross for over forty years. He owned the Norcross Drug Store along South Peachtree Street in the downtown area and purchased, with his wife and family, a home at 282 Thrasher Street, a property whose deeds can be traced prior to 1917 but not verified. The home's current owner, Mark Price, the professional basketball player who began his career at Georgia Technical University in the 1980s, did extensive research on the property after finding a collection of medicinal bottles around the home and unearthed as he landscaped the backyard. Extensive remodeling of the old home revealed many intriguing areas, like spacious dormers that were enclosed by walls, four original fireplaces, heart pine floors, beveled waves of windowpanes and an old telephone box embedded into a wall in the back hallway. Price rescued two mantels from the home of Noye Nesbit, just south of his, before it was demolished and they grace the fireplaces of the dining room and master bedroom.

Despite the well-intended doctoring of the day, weathered tombstones denote birth and death dates, often the same day, of those souls who departed this earth prematurely. Uncontrolled contagious diseases, unattended childbirth, an ill-timed crossing of a train track, farm equipment mishaps and a bloody Civil War contributed to the snuffing out of many a young life.

Just north of the purchased family plots at the city cemetery lies the unmarked bone yard of long departed Norcross indigents who died without the financial means for a proper burial or family plot in which their bodies could be interred. Bulldozed by the city many decades ago to make space for a youth football field, an undocumented number of impoverished remains buried there over time were never respectfully relocated or even properly marked. Only an occasional smooth rock bears witness to the dirt dump of the dirt poor. Souls of meager earthly means, some without benefit of a pine box, rest wrapped only in blankets and their death clothes somewhere below the crust of the overgrown rocky field, unbeknownst to fans who cheer a favored player just a short pass or punt away.

Nuggets of Nostalgia

The Norcross City Cemetery is the resting place for many first families. A paupers' grave was just to the right of this more tended area. *Courtesy of the Nesbit family.*

One-time millionaire Edward Buchanan left this earth with less than $100 to his name. By the mercies of many Norcross groups, he enjoys a coffin and stone under the trees of the Norcross city cemetery.

Tucked below the gazebo in Thrasher Park, a stone plaque acknowledging a young Norcross man lost in war is visible only to those who, with some knowledge of its location, seek to discover it. Harold Mitchell, born in 1922, died June 6, 1944, a casualty of the D-Day invasion into Normandy, France. The marker (not a grave) sits under a large, low-hanging tree in the northwest corner of the park in honor of a town hero whose body never returned home.

Hollis Rochester, once a fine athlete, was discovered dead close to the tracks by the depot. Many who saw his bloody body did not believe that he met his maker as a result of being hit by a train; it seemed more likely to those eyewitnesses that he had been dumped along the tracks to make it appear as though he had been struck by a train, possibly an effort to cover up the true nature of his demise. Some talked of vigilante justice or possible murder in response to Hollis's rumored thievery.

In 1922, tragedy cut short the career of one Norcross baseball player. Wyatt "Mike" Davenport was fatally injured while playing for Georgia Military College in a game against Georgia Tech. After colliding with another player as they both ran to field a fly ball, the young man from Norcross fell to the ground and never regained consciousness. The marching field at the college is named in Davenport's honor.

Remembering Norcross

Norcross saw its share of tremendous train wrecks, often leading officials to close some of the many crossings that were once in the downtown district. *Courtesy of Evelyn Norman.*

In 1945, John de Jarnette drowned at a beach in Florida. Lizzie Bishop went under at the same beach just five years later.

Also in 1945, a slow-moving train carried the body of Franklin D. Roosevelt from Warm Springs, Georgia, through Norcross, northward to lie in state at the Capitol Rotunda in Washington, D.C.

An un-gated railroad crossing at Wingo and Rakestraw Streets was closed after it took the lives of two people attempting to cross it in an automobile, only to be struck by an oncoming train.

The historic Mount Carmel Methodist Church cemetery is the final resting place of the first white child born in Atlanta in the earliest of days, when the city was known as Terminus.

As recently as 1991, Hopewell Baptist Church respectfully moved some illegible slave graves to expand its complex, under controversy and public fear of poltergeists.

Scattered behind the modern development of strip malls, subdivisions and industrial parks, hidden in churchyards, fenced family plots and city cemeteries, the relics of stone-walled wells, wood-slat barns, stoic hardwoods and crumbling, weathered tombstones tell a fading tale of Norcross's most colorful characters.

About the Author

Sally Toole began writing for her high school newspaper and later earned a scholarship as editor of the *Open Door* at DeKalb College in 1980. Working as a stay-at-home mother, child-care provider and teacher, she continued writing freelance articles for *Georgia Outdoor News* and *Creative Loafing* magazines. When asked in 2001 to write monthly columns for her church, the collection of devotionals grew into a book entitled *A Home for All Seasons*, which she published in 2006. A second book, *The Best Gift I Never Opened*, is a childhood memory of a wonderful whimsical Christmas. The story received an Honorable Mention at the 2007 Do It Yourself Book Festival, with a portion of proceeds benefiting animal rescue services.

Currently, Sally contributes articles to *Georgia Backroads*, *Woman's World*, *Mature Living*, *Norcross Weekly* and is on staff at *Inside Gwinnett* magazine. Sally helped begin and lead a weekly "lap sit" story hour, teaches summer vacation bible school and visits classrooms to speak with students about the writing process.

Sally writes for both the annual Haunted Norcross Ghost Tours and the Historic Norcross Holiday Tour of Homes. She is a member of the Norcross Historic Preservation Society, and has been instrumental in commemorating an Indian bent tree in Stone Mountain, Georgia.

Please visit us at
www.historypress.net

www.ingramcontent.com/pod-product-compliance
Lightning Source LLC
Chambersburg PA
CBHW060811100426
42813CB00004B/1031